Foreword
By the Revd Joan Watson

I arrived in St Agnes in July 2006, and what a privilege it has been to be part of such a caring, generous community! Part of this tremendous blessing has been to come and walk alongside the people of this village and become part of their story. Special thanks must go to Tony and Clive for putting together in words and pictures the history of Methodism here in St Agnes.

Showing how God inspires and blesses ordinary people down through the centuries is a source of constant joy as we reflect on those folk past and present who have given of themselves willingly and so unstintingly to bring God's Kingdom to their families, friends and neighbours.

Over the years the Methodist Church has been responsible for much that is good in this country and abroad. Therefore mission continues to be at the heart of our faith ~ reaching out in real ways and meeting specific needs within the village and surrounding areas to both old and young alike.

As you read this book I pray that you will see God's hand at work down the ages. I pray too that His story will be seen in the story of the Methodist Church here in St Agnes, and that God's Spirit will encourage, inspire and challenge you through the dedication and commitment of local men, women and children who have been faithful in His service over the last 250 years.

Your love, Lord God, accepts us as we are.
You see us through the eyes of love and forgiveness
as you challenge us to become more like Jesus.

In this quiet time, as we read these pages,
renew and refresh us so that together
with one another we can spread your love around.

Show us how that through us
someone may catch a glimpse of your love
And so find an open door into Your Kingdom.

Every blessing to you all

'I rode to St Agnes'*

Clive Benney and Tony Mansell

* John Wesley, September 2nd 1757

First published May 2010 by
Trelease Publications

15 Kerensa Gardens
Goonown
St Agnes
Cornwall
TR5 0YX

Design by Daniel Benney
www.danielbenney.co.uk

ISBN 978-0-9545583-8-3

Printed by R. Booth Ltd
Printers and Bookbinders
The Praze
Penryn
Cornwall
TR10 8AA

Contents

Introduction

The 150th anniversary of St Agnes Chapel is reason enough for a commemorative book but the decision to widen the subject base has enabled us to include what went before, at Goonown and elsewhere in the parish. It is an intriguing story, much older than the history of the building that we now celebrate.

St Agnes Methodist Chapel, or Big Chapel as it is affectionately known, stands majestically between the summits of Rosemundy Hill and British Road, a testament to those men of faith who decided that a new place of worship was required in the heart of the village.

It is a large building and nowhere is the size more apparent than from the lower areas of the village. It dwarfs the other buildings, its single eye gazing to the east, as if attempting to maintain good order in this busy community.

It was in 1860 that the foundation stone was laid and in the intervening time the building has witnessed both joy and sadness. If it could speak then it would no doubt tell of the happy occasions: the weddings, christenings, anniversaries and harvest festivals that have taken place under its roof. It could also recall the funerals and, on a wider front, the many local people who have gone to war in the name of freedom. It might also reflect that it is still happening.

If we consider the story of religion in Cornwall, or even in St Agnes, then the history of St Agnes Chapel occupies only a small proportion of that time, probably less than ten per cent. The Chapel is, of course, the main aspect of this book but it would be a strange story that did not start at the beginning, so we commence with some of the events before the day in July 1860 when the foundation stone of St Agnes Wesleyan Chapel was set in place.

Our thanks go to Betty Tredinnick, Joan Watson and the other members of the steering committee – Brian Roberts, Derek Skinner and Glynis Teagle. They have provided us with information, guidance and have cast their collective eye over the finished article. The Revd Joe Ridholls has also been on hand to help with the religious history and, of course, like many others, to provide his memories of Methodism in St Agnes Parish.

The Religious Landscape

The complete story of early religion is beyond the scope of this book but it seems appropriate to consider its changes as it moved across the centuries to the present day, through the periods dominated by Catholicism and the Church of England to the formation of the Methodist movement in the 18th century.

"...we the Cornish, whereof certain of us understand no English, do utterly refuse the new service."

The famous phrase that came in response to the Act of Uniformity.

In the sixth century AD England embraced the Catholic faith and the nation came under the religious jurisdiction of the Holy Roman Church. It spread across this island; gradually penetrating the Southwest and the little Celtic country of Cornwall. Catholicism was to rule supreme for almost a thousand years and adherent countries deferred to the Pope on all religious matters.

When Henry VIII took the throne he initially defended Catholicism but to achieve his marital ambitions and to seize the wealth from the monasteries he split from Rome and formed the Church of England. This did not immediately signify a move away from a Catholic form of service; England had simply removed itself from the Pope's influence and placed Henry at the head of its Church.

The next 50 years or so were traumatic. Depending on the viewpoint of succeeding monarchs, the country fluctuated between Catholicism and Protestantism with grave consequences for the more prominent adherents of each persuasion. Like the rest of the country, Cornwall was affected by the changes but despite the consequences many churches continued as before with the Catholic Mass and rituals. It is probable that for the ordinary worshipper in St Agnes there was little immediate change.

During the reign of Edward VI (1547 – 1553) it was the Catholics who were persecuted and the Act of Uniformity brought to a head the unrest that had existed since the beginning of the Reformation. It prohibited the Roman Catholic Mass and enforced the use of the first English Prayer Book. Very few Cornish people could read or understand Latin but the Mass was familiar to them and they saw no reason to change their style of worship. Apart from the religious changes the new prayer book had not been produced in the Cornish language and this infuriated many of the people. It prompted a rebellion and from this came the famous phrase, "We will not receive the new service, because it is but a Christmas game. We will have our old service of Matins, Mass, Evensong and Procession as it was before; and we the Cornish, whereof certain of us understand no English, do utterly refuse the new service."

The Prayer Book Rebellion of 1549 was swiftly and ruthlessly put down. John Wynslade, Lord of Mithian Manor, was one of the leaders who paid the ultimate price for his involvement. It marked the end of Cornish resistance and the beginning of the demise of the Cornish language.

Edward VI reigned for only six years. When he died, a Protestant, Lady Jane Grey, was declared Queen but she ruled for only a few days before Catholic Mary took her place. Mary's five-year reign was traumatic and by the time she died, in 1558, she had taken England away from Protestantism and back to the old religion – Catholicism. Bloody Mary, as she was dubbed, executed many hundreds of Protestants during her short reign but this renewed obedience to the Church of Rome was short-lived. When Mary died Queen Elizabeth followed her half-sister to the throne. Initially she took a more moderate line before leading the country firmly into the Protestant fold.

The Stuart period of the 1600s was Protestant but with an increased level of Catholic tolerance. Charles I married a French Catholic and many feared that he secretly planned a move back to Rome. But the new

Mithian Manor the home of John Wynslade. Photo taken in the 1970s prior to renovations being carried out.

A good sword and a trusty hand!

A faithful heart and true!

King James's men shall understand

What Cornish lads can do!

The opening lines of R S Hawker's poem "The Song of the Western Men" more popularly known by the title of "Trelawny".

religion was now on a firm footing and even in conservative Cornwall people sprang to its defence when James II introduced new measures to relax the laws against Catholics. They showed this through their support for Bishop Trelawny's resistance to the proposals; but for that "uprising" it is doubtful that many would remember his name. It is ironic that this non-rebellion looms larger in Cornish memories than the actual rebellion that cost so many lives and affected our history, thanks largely to the lasting popularity of R S Hawker's poem.

During the 1700s many Cornish folk felt neglected by the Church of England. The perception was that it catered for the upper classes but not for the working miner and labourer. There were, of course, various groups of Dissenters to which those who disagreed with the policies of the Church of England could turn. Originally these included Protesting Catholics but later applied specifically to Congregationalists and Baptists – the nonconformists. Clearly, dissent was possible but the state did its best to make life difficult for those who chose that path.

Many from the labouring class lived in poverty, often in conditions unfit for animals. On paydays men were likely to drink their earnings in the taverns on their way home from work, leaving little money for food and other essentials. Life was harsh with little relief in this world and no hope of redemption in the next. There were those who saw the need for change; among them were the founders of what became known as Methodism.

Methodism began as a Christian movement within the Church of England. It traces its roots to the 1730s, to John and Charles Wesley and to George Whitefield, the itinerant open-air preacher. All three were evangelicals and members of what was dubbed the "Holy Club" at Oxford University. They considered the Anglican Church to be apathetic and in need of revival but they were not Dissenters, they were firmly of the established Church of England, simply trying to change it from within in much the same way as the Puritans had attempted to do a couple of hundred years before. Indeed, many of the early meetings were held at times which made it possible for people also to attend services at their local church.

John Wesley's "experience" in May 1738 was to change his outlook and have a profound affect on future Methodism. He said, "I felt my heart strangely warmed. I felt that I did trust in Christ, Christ alone, for salvation."

It was George Whitefield who persuaded the reluctant John Wesley to preach in the open air, to reach out to those who did not attend church. Wesley did so in 1739 and became convinced that it was the way forward. People flocked to the burgeoning movement but despite its popularity Wesley continued to see it as a part of the Church of England. It would remain so until after his death.

John Wesley

John Wesley began to appoint lay preachers, a feature that was to become embedded in Methodism; wherever they went they preached to large crowds. Hymn singing was encouraged and those written by Charles Wesley and others quickly proved popular. This was accompanied by enthusiastic sermons which often brought accusations of fanaticism.

The movement might well have foundered early in its life when a fundamental difference of doctrinal opinion led to a split between the early leaders. Whitefield adhered to the Calvinistic belief in predestination propounded by John Calvin (1509 – 1564). It held that God elects some to be saved and some to be damned; stating that all are naturally sinful and unable to redeem themselves by their own actions. The Wesleys, however, aligned themselves to Arminianism, the teachings of Jacobus Arminius (1560 – 1609), which held that salvation is attainable by all through the mercy of God. It placed faith as an essential condition of salvation and these four emphases remain a part of the Methodist tradition:

All need to be saved
All may be saved by grace through faith
All can know that they are saved
All can be saved to the uttermost

As the Revd Colin Short so succinctly put it, "We believe Christ died for all and all can be saved." The debate had been rumbling on in the Protestant Church for almost 200 years.

From the early days the opponents of the "Holy Club" used the term Methodists because of their emphasis on methodical Bible study and worship. The members celebrated frequent communion, fasted regularly and abstained from most forms of amusement and luxury. They were active in visiting the sick, the poor and those in prison.

Despite its initial derogatory meaning, the title "Methodist" was adopted and the first Methodist Conference took place in 1744. A short while later Wesley established the practice of preachers moving to a fresh circuit every year or so, another policy which was to stand the test of time. Although the divide was becoming wider Wesley still saw the movement as an integral part of the established Church and to emphasise this he declared that he would live and die an Anglican.

John Wesley died in 1791. Shortly after his death the movement split from the Anglicans and established itself as a Free Church. Wesley's influence was missed and without his governance the movement lost some of its cohesiveness: various offshoots began to spring up. We look at these in a later chapter where we refer to them as "The Strands of Methodism." There followed a proliferation in chapel building with each denomination having its own place of worship. Most were well attended at first but the subsequent rise in the number of

"...all must feel gratified on contemplating the moral effects produced by their preaching on the lower orders of society... where drunkenness has given place to sobriety"

The West Briton newspaper of 1814.

denominations divided the congregations and contributed to the surplus of places of worship and to their eventual conversion to other uses.

The early members of the revival movement had been drawn from all levels of society including, as we have said, those who felt left out of organised religion. In 1814 the "West Briton" newspaper reflected on the positive benefit of the new movement when it wrote, "Whatever opinion may be entertained of their particular doctrinal sentiments and of the appearances sometimes exhibited in their meetings, all must feel gratified on contemplating the moral effects produced by their preaching on the lower orders of society in the most populous parts of the county where drunkenness has given place to sobriety and Bacchanalian conflicts to peace and harmony."

Methodism quickly gained popularity in Cornwall, an area renowned for its sense of independence and nonconformity. Maurice Bizley in his book, Friendly Retreat, stated that in 1823 there were 12,891 Methodists in Cornwall; one in nineteen Cornishmen was a society member – the highest proportion of any English county.

Like today, there was a degree of resentment at outside influence as a letter from an unknown correspondent to the Revd Thomas Collins in 1848 shows. It referred to "The uppish men who come to Cornwall to preach" but concludes that "the Cornish are warm hearted and hold such ministers and win their confidence in extraordinary esteem."

In 1857 "The Mining Journal" showed its positive attitude towards Methodism when it said, "We cannot but confess the counties of Devon and Cornwall, the mining population most especially, owe much of their moral improvement, their domestic comfort and their present condition in the scale of society and happiness, to the chapel."

Like all movements, the Methodist body had its ups and downs and during the early 1870s the Revd Peter Prescott, the St Agnes Minister, wrote, "The population

> *"...the Cornish are warm hearted and hold such ministers and win their confidence in extraordinary esteem."*
>
> Part of a letter by an unknown correspondent to the Revd Thomas Collins in 1848.

has increased by 22,000 but after all the revivals our membership is 3,700 less." Perhaps however this simply reflected the changing population as the indigenous Cornish joined the tide of emigration to the various mining areas of the world.

In August 1878 the "West Briton" suggested that the Anglican Church had neglected the people and Methodism had taken its place. This seems to confirm that Methodism in Cornwall grew up in a religious vacuum, where the ordinary people found the established Church unwelcoming. It was owing to the persistence of Wesley that they returned to the religious fold, albeit to a different type of religion than they had hitherto known.

In 1893 the Revd W H Thompson, the Methodist District Chairman, refuted the suggestion that Methodism was losing ground in Cornwall. Nor, he said, was it losing its moral and spiritual force. It was the strongest it had ever been relative to the population, more united and in fuller sympathy with evangelistic and aggressive work.

During the 19th and the first half of the 20th century life revolved around the chapel, especially in rural communities. Youngsters were encouraged to become involved in the services, the Sunday school and the social events; the chapel was a major part of their lives. It is less so today and there are many who believe that communities are poorer because of it. Now, in the early part of the 21st century, there is a desire among Methodists to work ever closer with the Church of England. For some that means looking forward to complete integration, not back to the days before Wesley and Whitefield, but a partnership. For others, perhaps the majority, that day is still a long way off.

John Wesley and his influence in St Agnes

The Methodist movement began in the 1700s as a part of the established Protestant Church. Between 1743 and 1787 John Wesley (1703 to 1791) and his associates travelled to Cornwall thirty-two times. They were exhausting journeys of about six days on horseback, requiring frequent stops.

St Agnes Parish history has many references to the visits of John Wesley. He preached in the village many times and on one occasion at Blackwater. Meeting houses, or as Wesley preferred, preaching houses, sprang up which must have increased the feeling of belonging to a new movement. Most Methodists ceased attendance at Church of England services but some followed Wesley's example and chose to remain Anglican.

On his fifth visit to Cornwall, on the 5th July 1747, Wesley came to St Agnes. In his journal he wrote, "…rode thence to St Agnes. At two I preached to a large multitude of quiet hearers, many of whom seemed deeply affected; yet soon after I had done, some began to divert themselves with throwing dirt and clods. Mr Shepherd's horse was affrighted at this, and as one of them stooped down, leapt clean over him; the man screamed again, but finding himself not hurt, he and his companions poured a shower of stones after him. I rode soon after through the midst of them and none lifted up a hand or opened his mouth."

James Walker, the Church of England Vicar at St Agnes, wrote to the Bishop of Exeter to advise him of the gatherings. He said that the number of converts was no more than 50 but more were feared. He also said that some of his congregation were so incensed by the meetings that they tried to persuade him to call in the magistrates.

It seems clear that the people of St Agnes did not immediately take to Wesley and his teaching but just a few

> "At two I preached to a large multitude of quiet hearers, many of whom seemed deeply affected; yet soon after I had done, some began to divert themselves with throwing dirt and clods."
>
> Wesley's journal entry of 5th July 1747.

years later, in 1750, he wrote, "I preached…at St Agnes in the evening to a multitude not of curious hearers but of men that had tasted of the good word." He was in St Agnes again in 1755 and on another visit two years later he wrote, "I rode to St Agnes on the 2nd September 1757 and found the great man, Mr Donnythorne, was dead. His mother and sister sent to invite me to their house. After preaching I went thither and was received into a comfortable lodging with the most free and cordial affection. So in this place the knowledge of God has already travelled 'from the least unto the greatest.' In the afternoon I spent an hour with Mr Vowler, curate of the parish, who rejoices in the love of God and both preaches and lives the Gospel."

John Wesley continued, "Sunday the 4th September, I T (name unknown) preached at five. I could scarce have believed it if I had not heard it, that few men of learning write so correctly as an unlearned tinner speaks extempore. Mr Vowler preached two such thundering sermons at church as I have scarce heard these twenty years. O how gracious is God to the poor sinners of St Agnes."

The gathering of societies into circuits now occupied Methodist minds and at the Conference of 1748 all of the societies in Cornwall and a few in Devon were placed in one circuit. This remained the case for a few years but as the movement grew it became clear that something had to change; in 1765 Cornwall was divided into two circuits, the east and the west.

John Wesley made many visits to St Agnes – twenty according to Bill Morrison in the first journal of the St Agnes Museum Trust. On one of those occasions he is said to have stood on a mound in front of a cottage on the corner of Vicarage Road and Penwinnick Road; where Dales Garage and The Cornish Range shop are now (written in 1985). Afterwards he stayed the night in the cottage of Prudence Tredinnick opposite the Masonic Hall in Rosemundy.

Wesley's own record of his visit in 1760 stated, "The congregation at St Agnes in the evening was, I suppose, double to that of Port Isaac. We had nearly as many on

Tuesday the 9th at five in the morning as the Preaching House could contain." This statement makes it clear that the village had a preaching house of some sort by 1760 although where it was remains a mystery as Goonown Chapel had yet to be built. In his Chronological History of the People called Methodists, W Myles gives 1780 as the date of the first Methodist Chapel in St Agnes but this must be wrong considering John Wesley's comment unless, of course, he is making a distinction between a preaching house and a chapel.

Wesley continued, "Afterwards I examined the Society and was surprised and grieved to find that out of 98 members all but three or four had forsaken the Lord's table. I told them my thoughts very plain; they seemed convinced and promised no more to give place to the devil."

In 1762 Wesley referred to the death of the curate, Mr Phelps. He attended the memorial service in the Church and as it ended the rain and wind arrived. A crowd had gathered to hear him preach and he wrote, "No house could contain the people neither could I preach as before on the top of the hill; I therefore made a halt at the bottom. The congregation gathered round me in a few minutes; we were tolerably sheltered from the wind and the rain ceased till I had done."

It would seem that Churchtown was a regular meeting place for open air preaching with the more sheltered area of Peterville used when the weather was stormy. Small meetings were often held in people's houses or the preaching house while large groups usually met in the open air. Gradually, the societies built their chapels.

Unlike in some other areas, the established Church in St Agnes did not oppose the early Methodists. While Wesley praised the Anglican clergy for this he did record their lack of enthusiasm by saying that, "They were not really well disposed to their fellow labourers in the gospel."

Bill Morrison has left us a valuable legacy of local history and his list of members of the Society in St Anns (colloquial name for St Agnes) in July 1767 is a gem. Thomas and Mary Phill of Gunyearl are the first entries. Thomas was a tinner.

In fact, most of those listed were tinners although there is the occasional cooper, servant, smith, ropemaker and carpenter. Many of the names are still familiar to the locality and if it is of interest then the complete list can be examined at the St Agnes Museum. It includes five groups of four or five names under the heading of "The Bands," fellowship classes within the Society.

On the 30th August 1768 John Wesley was here again and wrote, "Called at St Agnes and found a large congregation waiting so I preached without delay."

Later, during his seventeenth visit in August 1776, Wesley wrote, "The passage through the sands (from Cubert) being bad for a chaise, I rode on horseback to St Agnes, where the rain constrained me to preach in the house."

The Butson family have lived in Goonown for over 300 years, from long before Wesley preached in the parish. Colin Butson recalled his mother, Alma, telling a story that had been passed down through their family. It was of John Wesley preaching in the open-air at Goonown: from the steps of their barn.

John Wesley's last visit to St Agnes was in 1785, when he was 82 years old. He preached at half past eight in the morning and recorded, "It was to the largest congregation I ever saw there." Within six years he had died and the leadership passed to others.

At the Methodist Conference in 1785 the circuit structure changed again. Cornwall was to be divided into three circuits: St Austell, Redruth and St Ives. St Agnes was to be a part of the Redruth Circuit. This would remain the case for the next forty years but in 1828 St Agnes became the head of its own circuit with 14 chapels. The Wesleyan Methodist Preachers' Plan of 1835/6 included Bolingey, Calestock, Cubert, Crantock, Goonown, Higher Bal, Mingoose, Mount Hawke, Mythian, Rejerrah, Rose, Silverwell, Tramble (probably Treamble), Trencreek/Tremper (probably Trevemper) and Trevellas Downs. (We make that 15 so it seems that one had been added during the intervening years. In a few cases the spelling may seem strange but it varies across the years.)

By 1839/40 Higher Bal was included as Beacon Chapel and Tremper was listed separately from Trencreek; Tramble had disappeared. All of the chapels met twice each week, some three or four. By 1847/8 Wheal Frances was included and in 1852 Goonbell (Wesleyan) appeared for the first time but only met every other week. By 1856/7 it had disappeared from the plan. The letter "W" on the plan referred to a service when the collection would be for the "Worn-out Ministers and Widows Fund" and the Plan of 1857/8 includes those preachers who required a horse to be arranged.

By 1863 the new Chapel at St Agnes was in use and the Preachers' Plan reflected this by replacing Goonown Society with St Agnes Society. The wording had also moved slightly up-market and instead of "Horse Arrangements" it read, "Plan for Conveying the Preachers to distant places."

The 1865 Plan includes Quay Chapel which gives us some clue as to when this Chapel opened, or perhaps, when it began to be supplied with preachers. It then becomes Trevaunance Coombe (perhaps they were not the same building) and Perranwell was added. Four years later Trevaunance Coombe is missing and Perran Porth has been added. Under St Agnes, probably at Goonown, there was mention of a Day School.

By 1877 the number of chapels for which preachers were to be allocated was down to twelve. Rose, Cubert, Crantock, Trencreek, Trevemper and Rejerrah no longer appeared, no doubt moved to another circuit. The Plans from 1888 to 1895 included Goonbell again and a new entry, the tiny Chapel at White Street, Mithian Downs. Neither held regular meetings and in the case of White Street, either the St Agnes or the Bolingey Trap was available to convey the preacher.

An interesting report of October 1890 includes the following facts about St Agnes Parish. (Cornwall Records Office MR/N/863)

Estimated parish population - 7,750
Total number of chapel seats - 2,490
Attendance at Sunday evening service - 2,350
Number of members of society - 749
Local preachers - 22
Musical provision - seven harmoniums and three organs

In May 1898 the Leasehold Property Return for St Agnes Circuit included a number of chapels for which the freehold had not been purchased; some were subsequently obtained while others remained under lease. At that time the lease expiry date for Bolingey was 1931 and Silverwell was 1972. Others had no fixed expiry date and were based on the practice of linking them to people's lives. This was the case in respect of Trevellas Downs where two people were aged 32 and one was 30. Only two people were referred to for Mingoose: one was in Africa and the other was not known.

The Wesleyan Removal Register for the years from 1889 to 1907 includes many people who had left the village to travel to other areas of the world. It listed their names, their position in the society e.g. member, teacher etc., and to which chapel class they had belonged. Many left for America, Johannesburg, The Cape, Sacramento and even India and it is likely that their departures were mining related.

At times two ministers seem to have lived in St Agnes and served the Circuit and Bizley suggests that in 1850 they shared accommodation, perhaps in a house in British Road, where Cleaderscroft now stands. A few years later they were provided with a house each.

In 1840 the membership of the St Agnes Society stood at 515 but over the next 30 years it fluctuated, usually within the range of 300 to 400. In 1964 it was 133 and is currently about 110.

Class meetings are an integral part of Methodist Societies. By the mid 1800s there were 20 or 30 in the various locations around St Agnes. Societies were made up of individual classes, intimate groups where individuals were encouraged to confess their sins to each other and to offer encouragement. The number of classes remained at or just below 20 for the remainder of the century but someone writing in 1964 said that by then it had dropped to seven. Today, Class meetings are still an important feature of Methodist life and there are four meetings regularly in St Agnes.

Love Feasts were once a regular feature of Methodist life. They provided an opportunity for sharing testimony and were a key feature of early Methodism. They are referred to in the Goonown Chapel records and a quarterly Love Feast is mentioned in the January 1906 minutes of the St Agnes Wesleyan Chapel. They have ceased in St Agnes but the Revd Joan Watson said that they are still a feature in some other areas.

Many local preachers emerged from the societies and in St Agnes during the 1890s there were 12; our unknown writer tells us that in 1964 there were still seven and now, in 2010, there are four from St Agnes out of ten active preachers in the Circuit.

In the amalgamation of 1902 St Agnes lost its position as head of the Circuit and became a part of the North Cornwall Mission which stretched from Padstow to Porthtowan. This situation prevailed until 1932 when the Methodist Union saw the various strands of the movement come together and St Agnes Wesleyan Chapel became St Agnes Methodist Chapel. The North Cornwall Mission was divided into three circuits and the first quarterly meeting of the new Perranporth and St Agnes Circuit was held on the 11th September 1934. That situation prevailed for the next forty years but in 1974 there was yet another change with the amalgamation of Newquay, Perranporth and St Agnes into one circuit.

> At the end of 1925 the Chapel had 140 members, an increase of seven during the year. Six people had transferred out, nine had transferred in and four had died (best not to try and do the sums).

Chapels in the Parish

In the book "The History of Christianity in Cornwall AD 500 – 2000" the Royal Institution of Cornwall stated, "In Cornwall, Christianity has embraced continuing post-Reformation Roman Catholicism, Congregationalists, Baptists, Evangelicals, the Society of Friends and the often confusing many varieties of Methodism."

Following John Wesley's death in 1791 the movement decided that it was time to move out from under the umbrella of the established Church of England; Methodism as an independent body came into being. Within one generation, however, the fledgling movement began to feel some of the strains and divisions that had been more or less contained during Wesley's lifetime and new factions began to appear.

The division into the various branches of Methodism is confusing and we would never have begun to unravel it without some help. We have dipped into many sources but three in particular deserve our thanks and your further reading if you wish to pursue the subject. The Revd David Easton's paper "A Brief History of Methodism in Cornwall," Ian Haile's book "The Next Chapter Cornish Methodism 1965 – 2005" and the Revd Colin C Short's book "How to get methodical with your Cornish Methodists." The last not only de-mystifies the subject but also debunks some myths that have grown up about Methodism. It is essential reading for anyone requiring a fuller understanding of its various branches or strands.

The Parish of St Agnes has many buildings once used as Methodist places of worship and in this chapter we have listed them, where possible, according to their initial denomination. It is accepted that all Methodist branches came under the heading of the Methodist Church of Great Britain in the merger of 1932 but, notwithstanding that, they appear here under their original grouping.

Some of the buildings have now been converted into dwellings or put to some commercial use. Some are still used as chapels while others have disappeared altogether and we are left to guess their exact location. We have chosen to include those within the civil boundary of St Agnes which has remained constant whereas the Methodist circuits have changed over the years.

There are a few at the end of the chapter that have no connection with Methodism but we thought it interesting to include them. There are no prizes for spotting any we have missed although it would be good to learn of them.

Bible Christian Chapels

The Bible Christian movement was formed in Devon by Cornishman William O'Bryan, the son of a Wesleyan Anglican. His application to join the Wesleyan ministry had been rejected but despite that he began preaching near his home in Luxulyan, only to be expelled from the movement for indiscipline. He was later permitted to rejoin but differences remained and in 1815, with the help of the Thorn family of Shebbear, he founded the Bible Christian movement.

It is difficult not to conclude that personal aspirations played at least a part in the setting up of this church but the movement quickly grew and the first conference was held in 1821. Within a few years O'Bryan had fallen out with the Thorns and moved to New York where he remained for a while before returning to Cornwall. The Bible Christians were particularly successful in rural areas and were strong across the south, particularly in Cornwall and Devon. Billy Bray was one of its more famous preachers and, like the Primitives, the movement encouraged the involvement of women. Members were often referred to as Bryanites or Quaker Methodists and for a while there was an offshoot, the Arminian Bible Christians. In 1907 the Bible Christian Church became a part of the new United Methodist Church.

Billy Bray (1794-1868)

Towan Cross Chapel (unknown date – not extant)
This Chapel or meeting house once stood in the field on the west corner of the junction of Trenithick Mill and the coast road; it was certainly in existence in 1838 when it appeared on the Tin Bound map of that year. It was set in what became known as Chapel Field and although there is no longer any trace of the building the location is still referred to as Bryanite Corner.

Wheal Rose Chapel (1824 building   extant as workshop)
This little Chapel, also known as Ebenezer Chapel, Rose Chapel, United Methodist Chapel and Wheal Rose Methodist Chapel, was built in 1824. It was simply adorned and comprised a single room for services and Sunday school classes. Tea treat processions were led by a brass band down to Williams' Creamery (almost to Scorrier) and then to the field adjacent to the Chapel. Occasionally, the event was held in the garden of Rose House, a 16-acre farm with an impressive house and a large kitchen garden which must have been a superb setting for the event. The Chapel closed in 1935, quite early compared to other communities. Two years later permission was given to sell it.

Zion House destroyed by fire in 1909

Zion House (unknown date – not extant)
We believe that this meeting house, in what was once referred to as London Lane, was used for worship in the 1840s and maybe earlier. In 1873 Thomas Wills lived there; he is listed in Kelly's Directory as a shopkeeper and the entry for his children on the school register gives their address as Zion Chapel.

In 1909 it was destroyed by fire and a report in the "Royal Cornwall Gazette" stated, "Some sixty or seventy years ago the building was used as a meeting house. In one of the floors of the dwelling house was a part of the pulpit used by Billy Bray and this interesting relic is gone for ever."

The Methodist Church of Great Britain

In 1932 the Methodist Church of Great Britain came into being. The Wesleyan Methodist Church, the Primitive Methodists and the United Methodist Church combined to form the new body: a significant event.

Back in 1836 the Protestant Methodists (1827 to 1836) had been incorporated into the Wesleyan Methodist Association (1835 to 1857) and in 1857, that Association itself had combined with the Wesleyan Reformers (1848 to 1857) to become the United Methodist Free Churches. In 1907 there was yet another merger. This time it was the United Methodist Free Churches, the Methodist New Connexion and the Bible Christians who combined to form the United Methodist Church.

In 1932 The Deed of Union confirmed the structure which still exists; Methodism established its place in the Protestant Church and confirmed the doctrines held dear since Wesley's time.

Cameron Estate Chapel (not extant)
Following the abandonment of the military camp on St Agnes headland at the end of the Second World War many servicemen and local families occupied the empty buildings. Faced with the problem of where to re-house them the local authority took a pragmatic view and recognised the families as council tenants.

Once the community was established both the Anglicans and the Methodists became involved. The Revd Joe Ridholls asked Councillor Eddie Tredinnick if a suitable building could be found for a Methodist chapel and was given the keys to an old store. It needed a lot of work but with the help of Albert Reynolds and Jimmy Olds a place of worship was created.

Regular services began and the Revd Joe Ridholls, assisted by Marlene Ball (née Skewes), Bill Morrison and

The Revd Joe Ridholls

Bernard Jones, established a Sunday school. He also started a youth club in the old NAAFI; this was eventually linked to the YMCA network. In 1962, when the Revd Joe Ridholls left the parish, the Chapel became an outpost of the Salvation Army.

Trevellas and Crosscoombe Methodist (1955 building – extant as dwelling)
October 1955 was a memorable day as the foundation stone of the new Trevellas and Crosscoombe Methodist Chapel was set in place, the first such ceremony in Cornwall for about a quarter of a century. Crosscoombe Primitive Methodist Chapel had been demolished for the war effort and Trevellas Downs Wesleyan Chapel was inadequate and in a dilapidated state so the community needed a new place of worship.

Mr G H Chilcott of Truro gave the site and the compensation received from the Air Ministry, together with a grant from the Methodist Conference, almost covered the building cost. Furniture from Crosscoombe Chapel was taken out of storage; the pipe organ, which had been temporarily used in the Wesleyan Chapel, was transferred to the new building and members of the congregation donated many new items.

Both the Primitives and the Wesleyans were to worship there and, of course, as both of those groups had been incorporated into the Methodist Church the new name became Trevellas and Crosscoombe Methodist Chapel. It was opened on the 9th June 1956 with a stage, kitchen, toilets and parking facilities which other chapels could only envy.

In September 1991 the congregation began to decline and under the heading of "The last supper," the "West Briton" described its closure. "Services will end at Trevellas and Crosscoombe Methodist Chapel with Sunday's harvest festival. Numbers have dwindled to a handful. Decisions will be taken about the future of the 35 year-old building which is in a sparsely populated area where last century there were thriving Primitive and Wesleyan Chapels and working mines. The Revd John Haley said, 'No one could have envisaged that today almost everyone would have a car and that there would be such a drop in chapel attendances throughout the country.'"

The Chapel was sold and is now a dwelling. Derek Skinner of Mithian recalled that some of the pews ended up in the Bodmin and Wenford Railway waiting room at Bodmin.

Some time later the Revd Joe Ridholls retired and returned to the area. He said, "It was 1994 and I reflected on the situation that most of the chapels between Perranporth and St Agnes had closed: Trevellas, Mithian, Silverwell, Callestick and Goonbell. From a religious point of view the area seemed like a bit of a desert. I remember chatting to Reginald Mullett who lived in a bungalow very close to Zion House. We agreed that something should be done and for the next five years I ran fellowship meetings in his home."

Methodist New Connexion Church

According to "The Next Chapter Cornish Methodism 1965 – 2005" this group was established in 1797 but it seems that it was not until the 1830s that a society was established in Cornwall. It was always the smallest of the main Cornish Methodist denominations. In 1907 the Methodist New Connexion became a part of the new United Methodist Church.

New Connexion Church, Rosemundy c.1910.

Rosemundy (1835 building – extant as Masonic lodge/hall) The Chapel was built in 1835 following a split with the Wesleyan Methodists at Goonown. General William Booth, the travelling evangelist and founder of the Salvation Army, preached there sometime before 1865.

The members held regular tea treats in the adjoining field and in July 1923 the "Royal Cornwall Gazette" reported, "The scholars of the United Methodist Sunday school held their annual tea on Saturday. Fine weather and the presence of St Agnes Town Band brought together a large number in the evening." Within a year, however, the Chapel closed owing to lack of support. The Wesleyans of St Agnes were quick to extend the hand of friendship: they sent invitations to all of the UMC members inviting them to attend a prayer meeting at the Wesleyan Chapel and to unite with them in their services.

On the 17th June 1925 the "Royal Cornwall Gazette" reported, "The Trustees of the old Methodist New Connexion have sold their Chapel by auction for £240." The Trevaunance Masonic Lodge of St Agnes had purchased it.

Primitive Methodist Chapels

The leaders of what was to become Primitive Methodism had no wish to form a new church but they had become disillusioned and wished to revitalise the movement in line with the ministry of John Wesley. In May 1807 Hugh Bourne and William Clowes held a camp meeting in Staffordshire which resulted in many converts. The Wesleyan Church refused to admit the new converts and reprimanded the two men. When they failed to cease their open-air meetings they were expelled from the Church. In 1810, when it became clear that they would not be re-admitted, the two men founded a new Church, the Primitive Methodists. It was given this name because of the leaders' declared intention "to restore the primitive enthusiasm and zeal of Wesley's ministry." Those who remained loyal to the original movement were referred to as Wesleyan Methodists. Nationally, the Primitive Movement was very large and played a part in the formative period of Trade Unions and in the use of women as preachers. Here in Cornwall the Prims, as they were often called, were relatively weak perhaps due to the strength of the Bible Christian Movement. In 1932 the Primitive Methodists became a part of the new Methodist Church of Great Britain.

Crosscoombe (1836 building – not extant)

The Primitive Methodist Society at Crosscoombe seems to have been formed in 1835 with a membership of 20. The following year it had increased to 60 and they were building a Chapel with a capacity of 210. The choir sat behind the pulpit and at the back of the Chapel the seats rose steeply, to accommodate a classroom below. In 1884 the building was redecorated internally and completely refurnished with new pews, a new rostrum and an American organ. This was replaced in 1927 when a new organ was purchased from Heard and Sons of Boscawen Street, Truro.

The Sunday school was added in 1908. Members of the congregation provided the labour to build it but the carpentry work was let to local carpenter and undertaker, Frank Piper.

In December 1935 a soprano singer was in full flow when an explosion stopped her in mid cadenza. The superintendents rushed outside to catch the perpetrators but they were nowhere to be seen. Little did they know

Crosscoombe Primitive Methodist Chapel c.1906.

Crosscoombe Sunday School tea treat procession Saturday 13th July 1907.

that the guilty parties were in the Chapel, concealing their smiles. With a plan that was clearly modelled on the Gunpowder Plot, Doug Mitchell and Jim Boundy had brought the concert to an explosive and premature finish.

Doug takes up the story. "We had a couple of bangers left over from Guy Fawkes Day and I made up a long fuse out of binder twine, candle wax and iron filings. We put the device under the organ loft and took our places in the audience. We waited and waited but nothing happened so we assumed that the fuse had gone out. We'd obviously miscalculated on our fuse design because suddenly there was a huge double explosion; it was much louder than we expected and fair shook the place."

The decision to build a Second World War aerodrome at Trevellas sealed the fate of the Chapel and Sunday school. It was considered that they would provide a landmark for German planes; moreover, when the runway was extended, the buildings were on the flight path: they had to be demolished. The Chapel was very active at that time and it was a great shock to the members when they were told of the decision. When it closed in 1941 the congregation joined the Wesleyans at Trevellas Downs Chapel where membership had fallen to around six. All the interior fittings, including the organ, were used there and in 1956, transferred to the new Trevellas and Crosscoombe Chapel.

Goonbell (1830s/1840s building – extant as dwelling)
The Goonbell Society was supposedly formed in 1846 but a paper entitled Religion in St Agnes said that the little Goonbell Chapel was built before 1835. Perhaps, however, that referred to the Goonbell Meeting House. In 1848 the Society seems to have faltered and closed through lack of support but just four years later it was reformed and it is said that there was singing and praying in the streets. This time it went from strength to strength.

According to J C C Probert the Society attempted to purchase some ground for a new chapel in 1884 but they found it difficult to raise the money and had to repair the old. The refurbished Chapel was reopened for services on the 11th January 1885. More repairs were undertaken in 1919 and a written account in 1948 said that it was hoped that electricity would shortly be installed.

During the 1940s the congregation declined to such an extent that the Chapel closed. Perhaps it was the shock of losing their place of worship that caused people to rally around as in 1952 it re-opened under the leadership of the Revd F H Sims Clapp, a supernumerary Minister who had moved to the area.

On the 16th January 1955 there was a huge storm and the building was severely damaged: the end wall collapsed from roof level to within a few feet of the ground and the rostrum was crushed. This seemed to signal the end of this little Chapel but the members were made of stern stuff and decided otherwise. It was restored, the rostrum from the old Chapel at Trevellas was installed and a much-needed schoolroom added. While

Goonbell Primitive Methodist Chapel c.1960.

the work was carried out the congregation met at Goonown Chapel. In August 1956 services resumed. Twelve months later, on Saturday the 27th July 1957, there were considerable celebrations as the new schoolroom was officially opened. Unfortunately, as with many small chapels in the area, the numbers attending declined and in 1983 the Chapel closed for the last time. In 1985 it was converted into a dwelling.

Silverwell (1842 building – not extant)
In his book Primitive Methodism in Cornwall, J C C Probert stated that the (Primitive) Society in Silverwell lasted from 1841 to 1883. He said that a Chapel for 208 people opened in 1842; it stood in a field on Mount Pleasant Farm, in the lane that runs beside the Wesleyan Chapel (the existing converted Chapel). The building closed in 1883 when Mr John Harris purchased it for five pounds.

Skinners Bottom Meeting House (unknown date – extant as dwelling)
This is on the left when travelling from the village to Ivy Chimney and may well have served the Primitives. The front section was a single room built with cob walls. It has since been extended but the original roofline and windows mark this out as a former meeting house. The single-storey building is now a dwelling.

Skinners Bottom (1837 building – unknown location)
This Chapel was built in 1837 but here again, we are uncertain where and it may even have been the Skinners Bottom Meeting House referred to above. Within a few years the Society was facing financial problems. J C C Probert in his book "Primitive Methodism in Cornwall" writes that during the mid 1840s a nine-week revival was held when some miners cried for mercy.

Skinners Bottom (1875 building – extant as dwelling)
In 1875 a new Chapel was built on a site down the lane on
the right after passing the Wesleyan Chapel in the centre
of the village. The project seems to have been plagued
with financial problems and in 1894 the Trustees had to
borrow £90. The Directors of the Primitive Methodist
Chapel Aid Association Limited, from whom the money
had been borrowed, were involved in lengthy
correspondence with the Trustees and it was not until
1924 that all payments on the property were complete.
Having finally purchased the property the Trustees
immediately sold it. It is probable that the building had
ceased to be a place of worship even before its sale.
Since then it has been used for egg packing, as a barn,
for manufacturing wind surfing boards and finally as
a dwelling.

The Primitive Chapel as a barn
before it was converted into a
dwelling c.1980.

Wesleyan Chapels

Wesleyan was the parent body of Methodism and it was from this movement that the other branches split. It was formed just a handful of years after John Wesley's death and always maintained that it was the true heir of its founder by referring to itself as The Methodist Church. It was not only the first branch of Methodism in Cornwall, it was also the largest and most widely spread, even after the major divisions of the 1830s and 1840s.

The Teetotal Wesleyan Methodist movement was formed in 1841. It had its base in west Cornwall and was principally founded on that one issue. It was short-lived and most of its congregations joined the Wesleyan Association or the Methodist New Connexion. Nevertheless, temperance long-remained an important cause for some Methodists even though the early Wesleyans had been hostile towards it.

In 1932 the Wesleyan Methodists became the major part of the new Methodist Church of Great Britain.

Beacon or Higher Bal Chapel (1814 building – unknown location)
R Symons of Truro stated that the first Chapel was built in 1814 but his circuit record for 1825 stated "No Society" so we assume that it foundered.

Beacon or Higher Bal Chapel (1837 building – unknown location but possibly on the same site as the 1874 building)
The build date of 1837 and the recorded opening of the Chapel in 1842 suggests a lengthy construction period but it was a further seven years before the new Society was formed. The Chapel seems to have served the community for the next 30 years but in November 1870 it was seriously damaged during a storm. A wall collapsed and brought the roof crashing down. It was beyond repair and the members had little choice but to clear the site and build a new place of worship, possibly in the same spot.

The 1874 Higher Bal Wesleyan Chapel c.1906.

Beacon or Higher Bal Wesleyan Chapel (1874 building – extant as dwelling "The Old Chapel")
The new Chapel was completed and opened on the 18th January 1874. By the turn of the century the St Agnes Wesleyan Leaders agreed that the members at Beacon would be constituted into a separate society. In 1908 the building was enlarged and the event was celebrated with a tea and a public meeting. At that time there was no schoolroom.

Eventually the numbers attending fell dramatically and in July 1986 the building was sold and converted into a dwelling.

There was one little mystery that puzzled us about this Chapel; the date 1837 displayed on the gable. It was only after talking to Margaret Bonner in Chapel Coth that the reason became clear. The present owner discovered that a chapel had been built in the 1830s and he assumed that the 1870s date displayed was incorrect; he altered it to 1837. That was, of course, the date of the previous chapel which may well have stood on the same spot.

Beacon or Higher Bal Methodist Chapel (commenced before Second World War and completed after – extant as dwelling "Chapel Coth")
Frank Carpenter of St Agnes wrote that there were a considerable number of children living in and around Higher Bal and to cater for them a Sunday school hall was built. Following the sale of the 1874 Chapel it was decided to convert the schoolroom into a place of worship but its use was short-lived and it too closed and was converted into a dwelling.

Blackwater Chapel (Pre 1810 building – not extant)
It seems probable that the Blackwater Methodists first met in a small building attached to the Blacksmith's Shop, on the site where the Passmore Edwards' Institute now stands. The smith himself was a member of the Society and may have taken a leading role.

Blackwater Chapel (1810s building – not extant)
The first purpose-built chapel was erected in the second decade of the 1800s when Methodism was flourishing and congregations growing in what was referred to as the "Great Revival." The building was small with cob walls, thatched roof and was located to the rear of the existing Chapel building. It was basic and simply furnished with forms for the congregation and a desk for the preacher.

> Disaster struck in 1821 when Blackwater Chapel (1810s building) suffered a lightning strike and was destroyed by fire. The congregation had just dispersed and no one was injured but according to Thomas Shaw in his book "Methodism in Blackwater," one resident said, "'Twas no wonder the God Almighty should strike the Chapel weth lightnen, the people were so dead and dull!"

The 1825 Blackwater Wesleyan Chapel c.1908.

Blackwater Chapel (1825 building – extant as dwelling)
Following the destruction of their small Chapel the people
of Blackwater built a replacement. It was a little to the south
of the first and, as with so many Cornish chapels of this time,
local miners, farm labourers and tradesmen of the
congregation provided the labour; "The Cornubian"
described them as "Plain men of the village."

The formal opening took place in 1825. The Chapel had
an earth floor and the men sat on one side and the women
on the other, on uncomfortable backless forms. Tallow mine
candles provided the light with a number of them set in a
chandelier. There was no heating so in winter the
congregation's endurance must have been severely tested.

Additional space was soon required and in 1832 a gallery
was added and the seats let to those who could afford them.
It seems to have been the preferred place to sit if your
pocket could run to it. In 1841 new pews with backs were
placed in the centre of the ground floor with the few
remaining backless ones used by the poor as free seats.

The Sunday school was formed in 1837 and in the 1870s
two classrooms were built. These were either badly
constructed or inadequate as in 1889 they were demolished
and a new schoolroom built.

A harmonium was installed in 1859 and in 1868 oil lamps replaced the candles. To avoid visiting preachers having to use the stabling facilities of local taverns a coach house was added in 1874. To coincide with the Chapel centenary a new pipe organ was installed and two years later, in 1925, the Chapel was registered for marriages. Much later, Thomas Shaw described the Chapel as very plain with a battle-scarred roof caused by German action in the Second World War.

On Sunday the 28th April 1985 the Closing Act of Worship was held in the Chapel but at the auction in October of that year it failed to reach the reserve price. It was eventually sold and the building became an office, then an auction room, and finally a dwelling.

Goonbell Meeting House (unknown date – location known but no trace exists)
We have been unable to discover when this Chapel was built or if its initial use was as a place of worship. The first reference to it was on the Wesleyan Preachers' Plan in the 1850s but even then it only appeared for a few years. Of course, it may well have been in use earlier and simply not provided with regular preachers.

An entry in the St Agnes Wesleyan Chapel minute book in March 1903 referred to its dangerous condition. It was said to be so bad that meetings had to be held at Goonown Chapel. Matters were in hand, however, and by October members of the congregation had finished the repair work and the little sanctuary was re-opened. The Revd G W Thompson preached the sermon and in the evening the Revd W Hodson-Smith presented a lecture entitled "From Liverpool to Rome." It should have been illustrated but the lantern borrowed from Mount Hawke failed to work; it was said that it gave off clouds like a traction engine and filled the house with smoke.

St Agnes Wesleyan Society was paying the ground rent and cleaning costs in 1899 and probably earlier but in 1916 the payments ended so it is likely that the building then ceased to be used for worship.

Goonown Chapel (Goonown Schoolroom)
See separate chapter

Mawla Ancient Chapel (unknown date – not extant)
We have been unable to identify the original denomination of this Chapel and it appears here with the largest group, the Wesleyans.

Maurice Bizley wrote that the site of a chapel is shown on the Ordnance Survey map as being by the side of the high road to Menagissey, about half a mile beyond Mawla Farm.

In 1805 Lysons referred to the remains of an ancient chapel at Mola and in 1847 Mr Newton recorded in a paper to the Royal Institution of Cornwall that Mawla Chapel was 25 to 30 feet long by 16 feet wide and had recently been used as a cows' house. He said that the font together with all the other remarkable parts of the building were gone.

Peter Simmons of Mawla, whose family farmed the field in question, recalled pieces of foundation being removed from the field, appropriately named Chapel Croft.

Mawla Chapel (1842 building – not extant)
A new chapel was built in 1842 with seating for a congregation of 120. It was also the Sunday school which continued to use it when services transferred to a new chapel about 50 yards away. By the 1950s/1960s the building was considered unsafe: it was demolished and a new Sunday school built.

Mawla Wesleyan Chapel shortly after construction in 1908.

Mawla Chapel (1908 building – extant as Chapel)
By 1908 another Chapel was needed. The foundation stone was laid on the 8th July of that year and members of the congregation who had built it no doubt attended the opening ceremony the following year. The Chapel is still in use and in 2008 a new community hall was built next to it.

Mingoose Wesleyan Chapel c.1906.

Mingoose Chapel (1851 building – extant as dwelling)
The Society at Mingoose was formed in 1849 and two
years later the Chapel was built. The Sunday school
existed from the early days of the Chapel but during the
First World War it closed because many of the leaders
were away fighting. It re-opened in 1927 with Eddie
Tredinnick as Sunday school Superintendent. This role
was in addition to being Society Steward, Chapel
Treasurer and a few other jobs to keep him busy.

There were usually two classes – the little ones from
the age of three, taught by Mrs Carrie Yelland, and the
rest, including one elderly lady, Mrs Blitchford, taught by
Eddie Tredinnick. Mrs Yelland also played the harmonium
in the Sunday school and Chapel, unless some aspiring
musician wanted to try!

The Sunday school children didn't usually stay for the
3.00 pm Service except on special occasions such as
Anniversary when they performed their poems or sang
and received their annual book prize. They were also
involved in Harvest Festival helping to collect gifts of fruit
and vegetables and to decorate the Chapel, and of
course, attending the Harvest Tea or Supper.

The tea treat was held in July, in one of two fields below the Chapel, to which everyone returned after the procession from the Chapel to Towan Cross and back. A brass band and two people carrying the Sunday school banner always took the lead. At Christmas time the Sunday school party, complete with supper and games, was held in the schoolroom decorated for the occasion. Annual missionary meetings were another attraction and often the returning missionary arrived resplendent in some native costume or gave a lantern lecture on their work.

When the children reached their teens they were given a job – keeping the register, acting as Sunday school secretary, being responsible for the books, helping the younger children or even teaching if there was need of an extra class.

Although the usual number of those attending was between 20 and 30, except during the Second World War when the intake of evacuees swelled the number, the Sunday school undoubtedly had a considerable influence for many years as nearly every family in Mingoose and Goonvrea attended at some time until their children left home or school.

But sadly, as families moved away in the 1950s and 60s, numbers dwindled until only one family remained, the Murrishes. They attended faithfully until the Sunday school and Chapel closed in 1962. After that, only Sunday school Anniversary and Harvest celebrations were held there, perhaps for two or three years. The building lease was surrendered to the Enys' Estate and during the early 1970s the building was converted into a dwelling.

Some of the senior boys at Mingoose Chapel decided to have a little fun with a rather shortsighted local preacher. They managed to get hold of his glasses and fix a blowfly to one of the lens. They then spent the service in fits of laughter as he tried to swat it.

Mithian Wesleyan
Chapel c.1905.

Mithian Chapel (1836 building – extant as two dwellings)
Mithian Sunday school was in existence in 1815 so it seems
likely that a Methodist society had been formed there
some time earlier. In 1818 the Society had a membership
of 85 and a year later it is recorded as being in the Truro
Circuit but where they worshipped we do not know.

Mithian Chapel was built in 1836 and soon became
pivotal to village life. It was referred to as one of only two
Private Trust chapels in the St Agnes and Perranporth
Circuit, the other being Mingoose. It seems that there were
very few in Cornwall.

In 1911 Captain John Whitford of Rose-in-Vale donated
a new organ and John Tredinnick undertook the
installation. At the same time new seating was installed
and a general refurbishment carried out.

Tea treats in Mithian were once a major event in the
annual calendar. A number of locations were used over the
years but the field on the village side of Trewartha Farm
became known as Tea treat Field. Before it moved there it

was held in Moor Field, by the Rose-in-Vale Hotel. When it moved up the hill it caused some discontent and, under cover of darkness, Bill Brown and some friends moved the stalls and farmers' wagons, set up for the bandstand, back to the field at Rose-in-Vale. On the morning of the event there was the unexpected task of moving everything back up the hill to Tea treat Field.

The Chapel served the community for 150 years but during the early 1980s it closed and members attended elsewhere, including "Big Chapel" at St Agnes. The building was sold at auction and converted into two dwellings. The beautiful organ fetched only £35; there was only one bidder who just wanted the pipes.

It was probably a dislike for long sermons that led a group of Mithian lads to take matter into their own hands or more correctly, those of the Chapel clock. They advanced the hands in the hope that they would be let out early.

Mount Hawke Chapel (1820 building – extant as place of worship)

The Wesleyan Society here seems to have been formed in 1817 and, three years later, their Chapel was "built on a site in Banns, at a place called Mount Hawke."

In 1864 an area of the field adjoining the Chapel was purchased for the sum of five shillings (25p): this enabled a passage to be built at the south end of the Chapel, as a means of entry to the rear of the premises.

For many years Mount Hawke was a village with no pub. To explain why, we turn to the 1920 Wesleyan centenary booklet: "The cause of Temperance has always found a number of staunch supporters in Mount Hawke and it is probably owing to their implacable antipathy to the drink traffic that the village today rejoices in the fact that it is without a public house."

Historian Ashley Rowe called it the "Teetotal Village" when he wrote that miners returning from America in the mid 1800s, the old forty-niners, joined the Rechabites to form a lodge in their home village. At that time the Wesleyans were undecided in their attitude towards the movement but matters came to a head when the Chapel authorities refused to admit the Rechabites' banners and insignia. This opposition strengthened the resolve of the teetotal movement and it became all the stronger. Mr Rowe wrote, "The public-house, the Red Lion Inn, closed its doors (it was in existence in 1853) and although some beer-shops or kiddley-winks held out for a while, they too had to disappear."

The account of the Pub's last stand appeared in the "West Briton" of the 6th November 1863. "The last representative of John Barleycorn also practised the cobbling art but by some means or other, mine host found that leathering the sole and running the spirit was an unprofitable calling. From the best authorities upon the matter we learn that the evil eye of blue ruin was upon the house and the unlucky cobbler escaped from the malevolence of the monster by striking his colours in the night and hoisting 'Mr... shoemaker' the next morning. Since the occurrence of that interesting circumstance, no one has had the temerity to beard the 'Bogie' and things still remain in status quo."

In 1903, despite promises to the contrary, Mount Hawke Wesleyans decided to renovate their Chapel rather than build a new one. It took several meetings to arrive at this decision and the parties were so evenly divided that it needed the casting vote of the Chairman. But then, in a remarkable about turn, they agreed to build a new Chapel after all. The cost was estimated at between £1,000 and £1,200 and fundraising began but it did not go as planned. The 20th Century Fund would only contribute £100 and the Connexional Chapel Committee would only match it. Raising sufficient funds was going to be a problem.

It was probably finance that placed the scheme back in the melting pot and after a great deal of discussion it was decided that Mount Hawke would not have its new Chapel after all. Instead, the front façade would be re-built, the building renovated and new seats installed. In 1906 Mr Moyle of Chacewater undertook the work for a contract price of £700.

> During a particular dry spell two people set off for Mount Hawke Chapel to pray for rain. It must have been a true sceptic that observed, "It didn't show much promise, neither one of them had enough faith to carry an umbrella."

Monty Rodda of Mount Hawke had an excellent voice and was receiving rapturous applause and calls of encore for his rendition of "Old Man River" when an appreciative voice from the back shouted, "Never mind 'bout encore, let's 'ear n agin."

The Chapel is still active and in 2009 the schoolroom was refurbished for the benefit of the whole community.

Porthtowan (unknown location)

It is claimed that Methodism in Porthtowan has existed since 1796, maybe earlier if we include Aunt Betty Chegwin's open-air classes in Tom Tonkin's garden.

The Revd Thomas Shaw's book, "Foolish Dick and his Chapel at Porthtowan," describes the events that led to the creation of the Society and the building of the Chapel in a location now some distance from what we think of as the village centre. The Society seems to have been an extension of the one at Bridge, a small village not far along the road towards Portreath. Thomas Shaw said a young Methodist and mine manager, Thomas Garland, arranged the use of a cottage belonging to Tom Tonkin, the middle of a row of thatched cottages just below where the Chapel now stands. If ever that was not convenient then they could meet in Tom's garden under a cherry tree where Betty Chegwin held her meetings. He wrote, "The first class was held on the 26th February 1796 and its members were mostly elderly women."

Porthtowan (1820 building – extant as place of worship)

It was not until 1820 that the first Chapel was built. Thomas Shaw records that Aunt Betty Chegwin attended the opening and he is certain that Captain Garland and Dick Hampton (Foolish Dick) would also have been there.

This article in the Falmouth Express of the 20th October 1838 refers to Revival Meetings and it shows that not everyone valued them. "We are informed that what is called a Revival of Religion has occurred among the Wesleyans Methodists at Port-Towan, in consequence of

Former Mount Hawke resident, John Jotcham, provided us with a dubious sounding story about a preacher there. The man was sounding forth about Moses striking the stone and bringing forth water when he noticed some girls giggling. In an attempt to admonish them he said, "It's all very well for you girls to sit there laughing but you couldn't make water if you tried."

Dick never missed the services and classes when he was at home and was once heard to say, "I shud like to be consedered a Member of the Society in Porth Towan so long as I do live."

which about 70 have been added to the Society. We rejoice at the spread of religion everywhere but, having paid much attention to the subject of revivals, we have formed so decided an opinion of their hurtful effects, that we are always sorry to hear them."

Porthtowan (1841 building – not extant)
By 1841 a larger Chapel was needed and voluntary labour was used to build it – just behind the 1820 structure which was left in place. It was opened on the 30th May 1841. Three services were held in the new Chapel on the opening day and we are told that hundreds were left outside. Such was the interest that, "Wm Arnold preached in the old Chapel at the same time."

    Thomas Shaw said, "The Chapel had a narrow gallery, reached by steep steps from the porch at either end. Its original appearance was altered when the body of the Chapel was re-pewed towards the end of the nineteenth century. Open pews removed from a closed Chapel then replaced the original high-backed box pews. At the same time the small pulpit was replaced by a rostrum which reached the full width of the building. The old pews were retained in the gallery and a row of wooden coat pegs, formerly in the 1820 Chapel, was fixed behind the back pews under the gallery." Here again, a fuller description is included in Thomas Shaw's book.

The little 1820 Chapel nestles under the shadow of the larger Chapel which stood on the site of the present car park from 1841 - 1978.

The chapels stood, side by side, on land which had been a part of the Bassett estate; it was originally held by lease but in 1941 the Trustees purchased the freehold.

At a time when many local chapels were closing through diminishing congregations Porthtowan faced a different sort of problem: the 1841 building was becoming unsafe and so in 1977 it closed and services reverted to the 1820 Chapel.

Porthtowan (1980 building – extant as place of worship)
In January 1979 the "West Briton" reported that the 137 year-old Chapel had been demolished. The area where the old building stood was to be a car park and plans for a new Methodist Church of Great Britain had been submitted to Carrick District Council. Construction work progressed well during the summer and on the 12th January 1980 the new Chapel was opened. It was 20 metres by 7.5 metres with facilities suitable for a range of community events. The original 1820 Chapel was left in place, linked to the new by a vestibule. Unfortunately the formal opening ceremony had to be postponed owing to gale-force winds which had interrupted the power supply; it went ahead on the 12th January 1980.

The Chapel is still active. It is proud of its history and, remembering the early meetings in Tom Tonkin's garden, its logo depicts a group of worshippers under a cherry tree.

Silverwell Wesleyan Chapel today converted into a dwelling.

Silverwell (1824 building – not extant)
According to Bill Morrison there was a Wesleyan Society here in 1817. R Symons of Truro stated that the Chapel was not built until 1824 which suggests that they probably met in a temporary place of worship or in someone's house. We have also found a report which suggests that a chapel with a capacity for 140 hearers was built during the 1840s but our feeling is that the earlier date is probably correct. By the end of the century the building was said to be in a dangerous condition and beyond repair. It was demolished and the material sold.

Silverwell (1900 building – extant as dwelling)
In the late 1890s a Form of Application to the Wesleyan Chapel Committee in Manchester sought permission to erect a replacement chapel on the site of the demolished building; it was to have sufficient capacity for 300 people. The application stated that there were 65 regular hearers out of a neighbourhood population of 200; they were said to be "Farmers and Labourers." No schoolroom was proposed at the time and the estimated expenditure for the Chapel was £325. The lease was for 99 years at a rent of five shillings (25p) per annum although the Trustees hoped to buy the freehold in due course. Permission to

open the Chapel was granted in November 1900.

The construction cost was less than estimated but a dispute with the builder, John Symons and Son, for "extras," rumbled on for many years. When it was eventually resolved the Society had to pay its own costs which meant that the building of a schoolroom had to wait until more funds could be raised.

Like so many societies, Silverwell Chapel was built and paid for by the Methodists in the village and there was much consternation when it was discovered that the Methodist Church Model Deed meant that the local Trustees were only acting on behalf of the whole Connexion. Edward Lawrence, a local dairyman, was often heard to complain, "They took it away from us."

The Revd Joe Ridholls, Circuit Methodist minister from 1957 to 1962, recalled Silverwell Chapel as, "A very good building in a beautiful setting although somewhat isolated. So isolated, in fact, that one minister from Newquay failed to find it and returned home." This was not always the case however; the lane that passes the old Silverwell Chapel and continues on its way to Whitestreet was once a main thoroughfare. It was the preferred route, in earlier times probably the only one, from Mithian to St Peter's Church for funeral corteges. So although Silverwell Chapel appears to have been built in a strange location it was once alongside a busy lane.

Communion must have been a bit of a problem at Silverwell. The Revd Joe Ridholls recalled that on one occasion the Communion Table had not been prepared. "Never mind," said one old lady, "we can have a nice cup of tea instead, 'tis the same thing, isn't it dear?"

A frequent visitor at Silverwell was Buster the terrier. He belonged to Donald and Josephine Forway and was a regular at the services. It was not unusual for him to leave his place and make his way up to the pulpit to visit the preacher. Donald thinks that it was his way of saying that the sermon had gone on long enough.

Silverwell Chapel closed in 1982 and before long it was converted into a dwelling.

One miracle that you won't find in the Bible occurred at Silverwell in the 1950s: changing the jelly into wine. Someone had forgotten to buy the communion wine. "Don't worry," was the response from one of the stewards, "I'll make a weak jelly and no one will know." Unfortunately, the Chapel was a few degrees colder than her kitchen and by the end of the service the liquid had been in the little communion glasses for quite some time. One by one the congregation raised a glass to their lips only to find that the upper surface of the wine had set and was sealing in the liquid below. Finally, with some determined shaking and with one great slurp, gravity won the day. The Revd Ambrose Payne could hardly stop laughing.

Skinners Bottom (1827 lease – unknown location)
The Shaw Methodist collection referred to the lease of
½ acre of land from the Manor of Goonearl in 1827. The
period was for 99 years with four shillings (20p) rent and
"with full and free liberty to erect and build any meeting
house or houses to be wholly used for Religious Worship
by the people denominated Methodists." Unfortunately
we are not sure which building or to which sub-
denomination this referred but as the Chapel below was
not built until 1869 it could have been an early Wesleyan.

Skinners Bottom (1869 building – extant as dwelling)
This impressive Chapel, built in 1869, stands at the
crossroads in the centre of the village. It seems likely that
one of the other buildings mentioned was used before it
opened its doors.

In 1938 outside toilets were being built but it seems
that there were problems and they were not completed
until 1942.

Low attendance in 1957 prompted a letter to all
members seeking their views. Its use as a chapel
continued for a further 18 years but in 1975 a closure
form was signed and the various chattels distributed to
other local chapels or sold. The building was sold for
£4,500 in October 1977. After two years of negotiation
the minutes record, "Manchester (Methodist Chapel
Committee) delayed things to get the new legislation
through to their advantage and the solicitors excelled
themselves in dragging their feet."

St Agnes Chapel
See separate chapter

Skinners Bottom tea
treat c. 1906.

Trevaunance Coombe Wesleyan Chapel sits below Wheal Friendly Mine in Quay Valley c. 1905.

Trevaunance Coombe or Quay (unknown date – extant as dwelling)
It is not known when this little Chapel was built but it appears on the Ordnance Survey map of 1880 and even before that, in 1865, was included on the Wesleyan Preachers' Plan as "Quay Chapel." Having said that, it is possible we are talking of two different buildings.

St Agnes Wesleyan Society paid the ground rent and the cleaning costs but the payments ended in 1920, suggesting that it had ceased to be used for worship by then or even earlier. In March of that year George Higgins received four shillings (20p) for removing the seats and taking them to Goonown Schoolroom. The building is now a cottage called "The Fragments."

Trevellas Downs (1823 building – extant as workshop)
The earliest reference to a chapel here is 1815 but we
have no information about the Society at that time.
R Symons of Truro, in his book "Revd John Wesley's
Ministerial Itineraries in Cornwall," suggests that the
Chapel was built in 1823 – but as he was writing in 1879
that may explain the disparity in the dates. It would
appear that the Society floundered, as Maurice Bizley in
his book "Friendly Retreat" referred to an attempt to start
a Wesleyan Society during the 1840s. It would seem that
even that was short-lived as records show that the
Trevellas Downs Society was re-formed in 1860 with a
membership of 26, mostly from the Mithian Society.
A record of enrolled deeds at the Cornwall Records Office
shows that in 1840 there was "a conveyance of a Chapel
on trust for the Methodists." This is likely to be the
building that still stands next to the St Agnes to
Perranporth road but whether this was the original
Chapel from 1815 we cannot be sure.

For many years this little place of worship served the
area. In 1941 the Primitive congregation from
Crosscoombe transferred here to worship and for the
duration of the war it provided spiritual comfort for the
airmen at RAF Perranporth. It finally closed in 1956 when
the new Trevellas and Crosscoombe Methodist Chapel
was built. It then stood empty for a while before joiner
and funeral director, Roy Bilkey, used it as a workshop.

Trevellas Downs Wesleyan
Chapel decorated for
Harvest Festival in1908

Whitestreet Chapel or Meeting House used as a farm building in the 1970s.

Whitestreet Chapel or Meeting House (unknown date – extant but derelict in a lane off Mithian Downs)
We have little information on this place of worship except that it appeared on the Preachers' Plan in 1888 and was still in use in the early 1900s. It later became a farm building and the ruin still exists.

St Agnes Methodist Society has provided visiting preachers at various locations including the Epiphany Home (later Trevaunance Manor Residential Home) which had an interdenominational chapel where visiting vicars and ministers could lead the residents in worship. The former home has now been converted into flats and is located down a short entrance drive at the top of Rocky Lane, near its junction with Trevaunance Road.

There was a similar provision at Rosemundy Home (now Rosemundy Hotel) for unmarried women who lived there for a few months before and after they gave birth; it became known as the mother and baby home.

There were also occasional services at Summer Lodge Residential Home (now closed and demolished) and services continue on an ecumenical basis at Mount Pleasant Residential Home where the Revd Joan Watson takes Holy Communion to any resident who wants to receive it.

Non-Methodist Denominations

Bethel Full Gospel Chapel (extant as dwelling)
Marjorie and Henry Jones ran a Pentecostal Chapel at
50 Vicarage Road, on the first floor of what was then a
cobbler's shop. Situated opposite the Miners and
Mechanics Institute the building has since been The
Cobbler's Kitchen, Miller Countrywide, Goldies and now a
dwelling. John Jotcham confirmed that it was referred to
as an AOG (Assembly of God) and that he attended on a
few occasions during 1944 or 1945. He said, "I think it met
for about five years or so with a congregation of not more
than ten. For communion the men placed their
handkerchiefs on the floor before kneeling on them;
someone brought a loaf of bread and the wine was
served in a tumbler."

Chapel Porth Chapel and Holy Well (not extant)
In his book "Friendly Retreat" Maurice Bizley quoted Lyson
from the early 19th century when he wrote, "Over
St Agnes Well in Chapel Comb is a plain Gothic building
of stone about eight feet wide in the front where is an
opening with an obtuse arch." It was built over a spring,
said to have healing properties, but by 1820 it had
disappeared, its stones having been used for hedging.
The Chapel itself is thought to have disappeared by about
1780 by which time it had contributed to St Agnes
religious life for a few hundred years.

> It was built over a spring, said to have healing properties, but by 1820 it had disappeared, its stones having been used for hedging.

  (A more complete history of these ancient buildings
can be found in Joanna Mattingly's article in the Journal
of the St Agnes Museum Trust volume 14)

Mithian Manor Chapel (unknown location)
Lake's Parochial History and W Hals recorded a free
Chapel at Mithian. They said that it had been converted to
a dwelling house, "Wherein God was worshipped in
former ages by the tenants thereof." This information does
not seem to have been well regarded by some later

writers as they have suggested that the Chapel was a fiction, although W Penaluna referred to it in 1838. There certainly seem to be no written documents of any Chapel but the Cornwall Council Monuments' records state, "Although OS could find no information about the Chapel, local tradition locates it close to Mithian Farm, and with a graveyard, and also speaks of a monastery here." It has also been suggested that the Chapel was a part of the manor house itself and the rear elevation and the existence of a room that could have been for such a purpose do support this.

An entry in "A Study of Celtic Hagiology" referred to an "Ancient Chapel at Mithian as late as the middle of the 18th century, remains of which were standing in 1843, but it seems to have been entirely demolished by 1847. This was the Chapel of the Mithian estate and the successor of a Celtic Oratory, perhaps of St Mevanu." St Mevanus or Meen could have been the Patron Saint of Mithian.

Hals, in discussing the presence of a free Chapel in the Manor, said, "Now libera Capella, according to the Canonists, is a Chappel, by the Licence of the King, founded and envowed by the Bounty of well-disposed Christians with Lands, Contributions, or Compositions, for their private Ease and Convenience in serving God near their own Homes, without being obliged to go far off to the Parochial or Mother Church; and such are called free Chapels in respect of their being exempt from the Diocesan Bishop's Visitation, and founded, as aforesaid, by Licence of the King of England, or Duke of Cornwall in those parts."

A report of 1820 makes reference to a Free Chapel and in the tything of 1842 there is mention of Church Lane which could relate to the field called Park-an-Eglos. There again, the road from the Miners' Arms to the Wesleyan Chapel was referred to as Church Lane so there are many unanswered questions in this interesting village.

Mount Hawke Congregational Chapel (1780s building – not extant)

The Chapel was in old Church Lane, between Gover and the old school, and was built in the late 1780s. It was the home of an Independent or Congregational body but abandoned when the new Methodist Chapel was built in 1820. It stood empty for some years but then the Anglicans used it as a temporary church and schoolroom until their building was completed in 1878.

It seems that the windows and roof were round and an old St Agnes guidebook stated that it was in the field (adjacent to the lane). In 1852 the Revd W Haslam used it after an open-air service (revival meeting). In August 1878 the "West Briton" referred to the large, comfortable Methodist Chapel and to the fact that the Anglican Church hired a place that was little better than a barn which brought ridicule upon them. Its final use was as a barn and in 1958 Ashley Rowe said that it was still possible to trace fragments of the path that led to it but before long all trace had disappeared.

Peterville Dissenters' Chapel or Meeting House (1770s building – extant as shop)

The surf shop in Peterville at the bottom of British Road has had many uses but originally it was as a Chapel of the Countess of Huntingdon's Connexion and was never under the banner of Methodism.

During the 17th century the state prohibited religious assemblies of more than five people outside the auspices of the Church of England. This law was to discourage nonconformism and to strengthen the position of the Established Church. The Declaration of Indulgence later relaxed the penalties and permitted non-conformist assemblies. When a second version of this Act was issued by James II in 1688 it was feared that it was a step too far in promoting Catholicism and Cornishman Jonathan Trelawny, Bishop of Exeter, made his famous stand against it.

Peterville Chapel or Meeting House on the corner of British Road.

The Act of Toleration of 1689 granted freedom of worship to nonconformists who had taken the oaths of Allegiance and Supremacy. This included Protestants who dissented from the Church of England such as Baptists and Congregationalists but not Catholics or Quakers. Nonconformists could have their own places of worship and their own teachers and preachers, subject to acceptance of certain oaths of allegiance.

The Revd Thomas Wills was the evangelical curate at St Agnes during the 1770s and to quote historian Maurice Bizley, "He did great work in St Agnes, his Church being often filled from door to door." He left in 1779 but financed the erection of a meeting house for the Connexion at Peterville "…for the benefit of the small flock of followers he was leaving behind."

The following year, on the 18th November, the Bishop of Exeter granted it a licence in accordance with an Act of Parliament. It was to be "set apart for a place of Religious Worship in which a congregation do design to meet as Protestant Devotees," a place of Religious Worship for Protestant Dissenters. It was a chapel for over 100 years but following its closure it was used by many types of business. (A fuller version of Bill Morrison's story of this little Chapel is featured in the third Journal of the St Agnes Museum Trust)

St Agnes
Whitworth Chapel.

St Agnes (Whitworth) Chapel (early 1850s building – extant as garage)

Dr Henry Whitworth was intent on caring for the soul as well as the body and built this little meeting house in the early 1850s. Located behind the old surgery in Vicarage Road it was used for prayer meetings for a few years before becoming a domestic garage. By coincidence the old St Agnes Manse was next door to this garage.

As far as Methodism is concerned, it is difficult to imagine a more complex history, especially as this is only an abridged version. The full story of the various strands is even more extensive and confusing than we have been able to cover here.

Despite the early divisions between the movements there were attempts to work together and to achieve reconciliation but, said the Revd David Easton, local opposition and doubts remained strong with many people. There were even instances where individual chapels acted differently from others within the denomination.

As regards the list of chapels, it is extensive but unlikely to be comprehensive. Alan Green of Goonown talks of the possibility of an old chapel in the valley below Butson's Farm, there may have been another in Mithian Woods and Two Traps Chapel seems to have been somewhere near Banns. There are probably others…we await the telephone calls!

Goonown Wesleyan Chapel (Goonown Schoolroom)

The inclusion of a chapter dedicated to this Chapel reflects the importance of the building to the community. Before 1862 it was the main place of worship for St Agnes village and even after services transferred to the new Chapel in British Road it continued to be used for Sunday school classes and for a variety of communal uses.

On the flyleaf of the Goonown Chapel Trust Account Book of 1838 is written: "Goonown Chapel erected 1790." The date is then crossed out and "or 1785" added in different handwriting and ink. R Symons of Truro records circuit information and from that it is clear that the amendment was made in 1863. The correct date is important. Tradition has it that John Wesley preached in this Chapel on his last visit to St Agnes in 1785. He wrote in his journal: 'At half-past eight I preached at St Agnes to the largest congregation I ever saw there', but it is quite clear that if the Chapel was built in 1790 he could not have preached there. Could it be that the date 1790 was altered on the account book cover to make the dates fit? Or was it because it was known at the time that John Wesley did preach there and therefore the original date of 1790 was wrong? We may never know, but it is quite possible that the great preacher did speak at Goonown Chapel.

We do know that the Chapel cost £500 to build and there were seventeen Trustees. It was located at the western end of Goonown Lane and was 75 ft. long by 66 ft. wide. Together with the gallery it had a seating capacity of approximately 300 people and when its use as a Chapel ended it was the largest hall in St Agnes. The original floor was a mixture of lime, ash and sand and a notice in the porch read, "Ladies, please remove your pattens before coming into Chapel." This was very necessary to avoid the floor being broken up.

"Ladies, please remove your pattens before coming into Chapel."

In 1809 a Methodist Sunday school was formed; it was to remain at Goonown for 130 years before it moved to the new Chapel in British Road where it still meets today. In 1862, the building ceased to be the St Agnes place of worship but it continued to be the home of the Sunday school and it increasingly became referred to as Goonown Schoolroom. The story of the Sunday school and its members is covered in a later chapter.

The record books of the Goonown Chapel Trust, held at the County Record Office in Truro, give an interesting picture of the early years of this Chapel. The earliest minute book, starting in October 1838, names the Chapel Trustees as Stephen Dale, James Angwin, James Evans, James Prout, Samuel Pearce, Joseph Ninnis, Francis Rowe, Stephen Martin, Thomas Martin, James Stephens, Edward Woolcock, Richard Rowe, William Rowe, Thomas Gill, Thomas M Ninnis, Thomas Rowse and John Nancarrow.

John Julian (born 1839) was considered to be one of the greatest ever authorities on hymns.

St Agnes man John Julian was considered to be one of the greatest ever authorities on hymns. He was born in 1839 and baptised at Goonown Wesleyan Chapel; his father was at one time a Wesleyan Minister. His Dictionary of Hymnology, published in 1892, will long remain the standard book on the subject.

On the 1st November 1851 the Chapel was registered for the solemnizing of marriages, and on Christmas Day 1852, Sol Paull James was presented with a Bible and hymn book on his marriage, it being the first solemnized in the Chapel. The name of his bride is not mentioned.

A spring cart was purchased in 1856 from Josiah Tregellas; it cost eleven guineas and was for circuit use. For many years the Society owned a circuit horse and soon after the purchase of one mare it was found that she was pregnant. In later years it was decided to hire a horse rather than have the bother of stabling and feeding their own.

Maurice Bizley referred to the lack of an organ in 1853 and to payments for a serpent and repairs to a bass viol. One of the largest items of expenditure was the purchase of tallow candles for lighting. Water was purchased at two shillings (10p) a year from a neighbouring well owner and the rent to the Duchy of Cornwall was set at two-pence. The cleaner had to be paid and he or she received £1 per annum while the door-keeper (perhaps the caretaker) was paid £1.10s.

We are fortunate that the Revd Joseph Whitehead recorded his memories of his time at St Agnes – from 1853 to 1855. Writing in 1879 he described the many aspects of his incumbency. Surely, the experiences of no other minister before or after him could compare to the trauma and poignancy of his initial few weeks – to the dark shadow that came over his domestic life on his arrival.

With his wife and their four children he journeyed from Ware to Plymouth by rail and from there to Truro by omnibus. He described it as a very hot day for travel. On reaching Truro they transferred to an open vehicle for the nine-mile journey over "bleak, open country to St Agnes" in the cold evening air. Joseph's two year-old son, Henry Rivett, was affected by the sudden change in temperature and fell ill with a severe attack of dysentery. He died within a week of arrival at St Agnes. A week later his wife also died, to be followed a day or two later by his nine-month old daughter.

Joseph wrote of his distress, his faith and of the kindness of Mrs Boundy in caring for his other two children. He also wrote of the kindness and skill of Dr Whitworth, a minister's son, who made no charge for treating his family (this was Dr Henry Whitworth, the first of the Whitworth doctors in St Agnes)

He referred to the great religious revivals in the Wesleyan Methodism Church and recalled one or two at St Agnes during his time there. He said, "The people yield themselves up to the spirit of excitement on these occasions and the effects are somewhat extraordinary. When a person is awakened by the Word and Spirit of God, and gives evidence of it, he is said to be 'taken down' and sometimes an individual so affected falls down in his pew and cries aloud for mercy."

He described the Sunday congregations as very large and the attendance at the weekday evening meetings as exceedingly good. He also preached on a Saturday evening to allow the miners the opportunity to attend. Morning prayer

"The people yield themselves up to the spirit of excitement on these occasions and the effects are somewhat extraordinary."

Joseph Whitehead comment on the great religious revivals in the Wesleyan Methodist Church.

The Revd Joseph Whitehead, St Agnes Methodist Minister 1853 - 1855.

meetings were at 5.00am, even in winter: this enabled the miners to be at work by 6.00am.

A typical Sunday for him was a mile and a half walk before 8.00am to meet four classes. At 10.30am he preached to a large congregation and then met two more classes. In the afternoon he walked a further two miles, preached again and met two more classes. After tea he walked three miles, preached to a large congregation and met four more classes. He then walked four miles to his home.

The Revd Joseph Whitehead described his house at St Agnes as a good villa residence. It was in a valley with a large garden and at the rear was a perpendicular rock with beautiful wild flowers growing at its base. He said that his circuit stretched along the coast for 12 miles and that he travelled on horseback to the most distant places. The Chapel at Goonown is recorded as a large, plain building.

He referred to the curious mode of calculating the minister's stipend. It seems that it was considered similar to that of a mine captain and the amount needed divided amongst the members.

The singing at St Agnes impressed him, particularly at Christmas. He described the tunes as peculiar, for the most part solemn and impressive, sung in a Gregorian strain.

Before he left St Agnes, Joseph remarried. Eleanor Ranson became his wife and mother to his remaining children – John Wesley and Elizabeth Whitehead.

The Revd John Jeffreys came to St Agnes in 1854 to join Joseph Whitehead. It seems that he wore his hair turned up in front in a cob and a number of his congregation saw this as evidence of pride and complained to Joseph Whitehead. He took the view that their own style of having their hair cut on their brows showed an even greater amount of pride.

John Jeffreys married while he was at St Agnes and Joseph Whitehead referred to his wife riding the Circuit Horse to improve her poor health. Some of the congregation objected to this and showed their disapproval in a less than Christian way: by mutilating the horse's mane and tail.

The Revd Frederick C Haine also came to St Agnes around this time and is described by Joseph Whitehead as an excellent man and a good preacher.

The Revd Peter Parsons was the minister from 1857 to 1860, presumably the last at Goonown Chapel before the transfer to the new building in British Road. His wife was Amelia Opie, probably the daughter of Edward Opie of Harmony Cot, Trevellas.

Goonown Chapel, with its congregation now worshipping elsewhere, continued to be the home of the St Agnes Wesleyan Sunday school. More space was needed in 1852 and it was resolved that a new vestry be erected for accommodating the classes.

At a Trust meeting in August 1867 the Chairman stated that two brothers named Oates, from Blackwater, had applied to use the vestry for a day school. Both these men later became headmasters at Blackwater Board School. It was resolved that they be allowed to use it on weekdays until 1869. The rent was set at two shillings and sixpence (12½p) per quarter.

In October 1870 the first public meeting was held at Goonown following the re-establishment of the Band of Hope.

As the world turned the corner into the 20th century the building was over 100 years old and in need of repair. The "Royal Cornwall Gazette" newspaper of the 14th January 1904 reported that Sir Edwin Durning Lawrence had given a donation of two guineas towards renovation of Goonown Sunday school.

In the first half of the 20th century Goonown Sunday school remained the centre for many activities in the village's religious and social life including harvest suppers, tea treats, concerts, pantomimes, bazaars and jumble sales. Frank Roberts recalled a bazaar in the 1930s when Captain Keast ran an indoor shooting range – with air pistols! He also recalled the huge banners which were carried at the head of the tea treat processions. The words "Strong Drink is Raging" and "Wine is a Mocker," were painted on the two side walls of the hall. Many concerts were held in the hall and in 1932 Truro People's Choir were the stars in a concert to raise money for Society funds.

Frank also recalled being a member of the Sea Scouts. He said that they had to go out in the road and come running when the leader sounded the bugle.

The Boxing Day concerts were wonderful musical events and always packed, according to Margaret Davey. "The best day of the holiday for the young people." Of course, in those days there was no television and for many not even a radio. The January Feast Day was always celebrated with a Faith Tea and concluded with a concert by the Chapel Choir. For Margaret, the Christmas celebrations were the highlight of the year. She said, "The Choir, of course, sang Thomas Merritt's carols in the Chapel and from house to house around the village.

Henry Jennings usually provided the lighting with a hurricane lamp."

During the late 1930s some of the youngsters asked if they could set up a badminton court and the Revd A G Payne led a team of workers in removing the stage and box pews to make room for it. Frank Roberts helped with the work but was "called up" before he had a chance to play on it. Sometime later a portable stage was built.

There is nothing better for fun and games than a flurry of snow, better still if it settles for a while. A group of lads had started rolling a snowball at Goonbell Halt and as they approached the hall the sound of singing reached their ears; it was choir practice night. Pity to waste all this effort, they thought. They trundled the, by now, large snowball towards the entrance and wedged it in the opening, right up against the door. There it remained until the end of practice. It was amusing that during the telling of this story Frank Robert's veil of anonymity slipped as he changed from a "group of lads" to "we."

The old Goonown Chapel ceased to be a home to the Sunday school from the outbreak of the Second World War, and in October 1940 local builder Albert Reynolds cleared the building. In 1943 there was a considerable build-up of troops in Cornwall prior to the D-Day landings and the empty Chapel was requisitioned for use as a billet for American forces. Margaret Davey remembers the hall being used by soldiers returning after Dunkirk and described many of the men as being in rags and tatters. She said that the inside of the building was left in a poor condition.

Camborne Town Band provided a concert there in February 1948. Pam Roberts was able to confirm the date; it was her second date with Frank. She said, "The first was the night before so it must have gone alright." Frank asked if the band could play Slavonic Rhapsody, a particularly rousing piece of music. The conductor, Mr A W Parker, said that they would play it if the roof could stand it.

Prior to the D-Day landings the empty Chapel was requisitioned for use as a billet for American forces.

In 1949, after some repairs and decoration, the building became the home for the new badminton club. It was also used for social events and concerts. Colin Butson of Goonown said, "This was the biggest public hall in St Agnes; it had a balcony and could accommodate large audiences. The stage was stored in a room adjoining the hall and erected for each event. The gallery was eventually condemned."

The 21st anniversary of the St Agnes and Perranporth Methodist Circuit was celebrated in the hall in 1955 when a 28lb birthday cake was the centrepiece of the celebratory tea.

Goonown Chapel today divided into three dwellings.

In 1963 Norman Coad purchased the building. He demolished half of it, the section bordering the lane, and converted the remainder into three dwellings. The metal entrance gates were removed and sold to Ralph Butson; they are still at Goonown Farm.

There are still a few people who remember the building as a Sunday school but most will probably recall it as a superb concert venue. Its use was not restricted to the Wesleyans; it was a community hall much used by many village associations. It is recalled with affection and had it been more central to the village it might not have been lost to us.

St Agnes or Bryannack Wesleyan Chapel

In May 1858 the Goonown Chapel Trustees withdrew the necessary funds from the Cornish Bank in Truro and purchased a piece of land from the Bryannack Estate. Their intention was to build a new Methodist place of worship in St Agnes (Bryannack being the ancient name for the village), in a more central position. It was a bold move and a new Board of Trustees was appointed to oversee the project. At their first meeting, on the 18th April 1860, they resolved to build the new Chapel.

And so to work...

Mr Richards of Redruth was instructed to produce a design; the Chapel was to be 65 feet long by 50 feet wide which, with a balcony, would seat over 900 people. Working with committees is never easy and we can imagine the deliberations over the sketch plans. Eventually, however, the design was agreed and Mr Richards was asked to proceed with the working plans. The project then moved to the next stage and tenders were invited from local building companies. The quotations were to be returned by the due date when the envelopes would be opened to determine who would be chosen to undertake the work.

Presumably there was no great surprise at the cost and Mr Abraham Delbridge's was declared to be the preferred quotation. An order was placed and preparations made for the work to begin.

We can imagine the construction team arriving with their horses and wagons, handcarts, picks and shovels, but apart from the lack of mechanical equipment the process would have been little different from today's

On the face of the foundation stone it read "AD 1860" and one wag suggested that the AD stood for Abraham Delbridge.

The disused Boddy's Quarry in Jericho Valley in 2009.

Some time later, a member of the congregation who had been using one of the "free seats" approached John Angwin to ask if he could rent a Chapel pew.
"Yes," said Mr Angwin, obviously keen on a bit more income, "where would you like to sit?"
"Well," said the man, "I quite fancy one of the middle seats at the back."
"You can't do that," replied an indignant John Angwin, "that's like going from steerage to first class in one jump."

except for rather less red tape. Mr Delbridge would first have examined the plan. He would probably have then lit his pipe, scratched his head and instructed his men to begin the arduous task of hand-digging the foundation trenches. The sand, aggregate and cement would have been brought in separately and the concrete mixed on site, once again by hand. The building stone was from local sources; about 670 tons was transported from Boddy's Quarry in Jericho Valley and a further 380 tons brought in from Polberro Quarry.

Every major building has to have its ceremonial foundation stone and Dr George Smith of Camborne, the Chairman of the Cornwall Railway, arrived on the 9th July 1860 to carry out the task of laying it. For the benefit of future historians a bottle was placed in a cavity within the stone; it contained the names of the Trustees, circuit ministers and the preachers' plan.

Over 130 years later, Terry Knight of the Cornwall Centre, Redruth, was browsing through a catalogue of items to be auctioned at Trevarno, near Helston, when he spotted an item of local interest: it was the silver trowel presented to Dr Smith when he laid the foundation stone way back in 1860. Terry immediately alerted the members of St Agnes Museum Trust who decided that this was an item that had to come to St Agnes. Since 1995 it has been one of their exhibits in the Museum at Penwinnick Road.

For reasons not recorded the building work did not progress smoothly. By February 1861 there were mounting difficulties with the contractor and eventually the situation became so bad that the Trustees paid Mr Delbridge for the work he had carried out and dismissed him from the job. We are not told of any subsequent legal dispute so we assume that the settlement was mutually acceptable.

The Trustees then took on the job of organising the remainder of the work. Various sections were let and it would seem that the project proceeded more smoothly. There was certainly no problem with the woodwork carried out by John Roseveor (or Roseveare) of Truro.

The silver trowel presented to Doctor Smith when he laid the foundation stone in 1860.

Undoubtedly there were a few more problems along the way but these were overcome and at last the building was finished. On Wednesday the 18th June 1862, about two years after the laying of the foundation stone, the new Chapel was opened. The Revd Richard Roberts of Huddersfield performed the dedication and afterwards about eight hundred people enjoyed a cold dinner in the British Road School.

The total cost of the project, including land, was just over £2,000. One gentleman had given £25 but the gift was conditional: if ever a Sunday school, tea meeting or teetotal meeting was held in the Chapel then the money was to be returned. The gift was accepted on that condition, and despite the subsequent breach there is no reference to any refund being made.

Maurice Bizley informs us that a fortnight after the opening the Trustees met to consider applications for the 103 family pews and we can imagine the level of diplomacy required in the allocation process. For the "free seats" it was resolved that the men would sit on the south side of the Chapel (Rosemundy Hill side) and the women on the north. Forms without backs were placed in the large vestry and benches placed against the walls and partitions in the upper vestries.

above; The earliest known photograph of the Chapel believed to have been taken shortly after it was built in 1860.

right; The interior of the Chapel c.1905.

Nine large camphene lamps were purchased to light the Chapel on the ground floor and ten for the gallery with two smaller ones for the platforms and two for the lobbies. These appear to have been inadequate as additional ones were installed in 1863. A font and table for communion was added in 1864 and two years later a cast iron chest was purchased for chapel and circuit documents.

The Grounds

The area of land belonging to the Chapel was far greater than is now occupied by the building and car park: it stretched all the way down to the little field opposite Cleaderscroft and included what we now know as Castle Meadows. The unoccupied parts continued to be farmed with any profit credited to the Chapel current account. Most of this land was retained until 1961.

The grounds had been planted when the Chapel was built but, after just six years, vandalism raised its ugly head. The Trustees met to discuss "the disorderly and disgraceful conduct of boys and others who were in the habit of entering the Chapel grounds on Sunday evenings during public services, disturbing the congregation and breaking down young trees and shrubs…" Action was needed. Notices were erected and Mr Richard Hooper of Goonown was asked to keep a watch on the premises. Perhaps this worked for a while but a couple of years later the Trustees asked the police to intervene. It seems from this that such behaviour is not just a current phenomenon.

The Chapel c.1906 showing the streetlight where the War Memorial stands today.

The land originally owned by the Chapel, now Castle Meadows.

A few years later, in 1873, Mrs Warne of Rosemundy busied herself planting trees and shrubs around the Chapel. Despite the earlier reports of vandalism she pressed on with her work and it is she whom we have to thank for the tranquil rural setting that is such a feature of the Chapel grounds.

In October 1907 some unknown person wrote this newsy letter; it serves to prove that nothing on this earth is truly new.

"I went to Chapel with Father this morning and we were all bundled up in the vestry as the weather was so bad and there were only a few people out. We had our first Guild Meeting last Friday. I don't know how the Guild will be but we have arranged a very nice programme. Have you heard about Fern and the others? It seems that all the lot of those boys were drunk last week and pulled up a seat down by Janie Quick's house and put it across the road. Anyhow, that is the yarn that is out. Fern, Alf Mitchell and one of those boys Tregellas (down Goonvrea) are summoned. Frank said he isn't surprised as they have been awful lately. One night they removed Captain Hooper's gate, laid it in the road and rolled those two granite balls down over Rosemundy Hill. Of course

The entrance to the Chapel c.1910.

these things are dangerous to the public but I don't believe that there is any harm meant. Poor old Will generally manages to keep his name clear but he belongs to the party."

At his first Trustee Meeting in 1969 the Revd Philip Williams recalled there being some concern regarding the state of the old barn on the edge of the grounds. Clearly the discussion had drifted on for some time when Miss Oates came out with the remark, "I wish someone would put a bomb under it." A couple of weeks later Philip was on his way home from a meeting when he came across some fire engines – at the barn. It seems that some youngsters had been inside setting off fireworks and had set it alight. With tongue firmly in cheek, Philip told Miss Oates that she had a lot to answer for, but the insurance company paid out and the site was cleared to make a garden and parking space for the Caretaker's cottage.

The Organ

In the Goonown Chapel chapter there is a mention of a group of musicians who provided the musical accompaniment. It is likely that this arrangement continued in the new building during the first few years of its life. Chapels were, of course, the birthplace of many Cornish brass bands and it is likely that a few local players figured in their number. Despite that, it is clear that the St Agnes Wesleyans were keen to have their own organ and in 1872 George Hele of Plymouth, the well-known organ company, installed a pipe organ at a cost of £170. It had two manuals (keyboards) with a total of 56 notes and a 25 note pedal board. It must have been with some pride that the congregation sang its first hymn accompanied by this grand instrument. Ten years later a few alterations were carried out: a new front was fitted, the pipes decorated and two stops altered.

Many young lads earned a few shillings by pumping the organ and in 1911 John Angwin paid out £1.10s per quarter for the "Organ and Blower." The amount seemed untouched by inflation as it remained the same for many years.

In June 1934 the job of pumping the organ at St Agnes became an item of history when an electric organ blower was installed. The boys would have to look elsewhere for their pocket money.

From time to time an organ requires some attention and in 1928 a fairly major overhaul and clean was carried out. It cost £47 and on completion the instrument was tuned for an additional £1.1shilling.

The famous organist Dudley Savage came to St Agnes in 1972. The organ had been in place for 100 years and he took part in the concert arranged to celebrate its centenary.

In 2002 the Methodist Organ Advisor, Philip L Carter, was asked to prepare a report on its condition. For over 70 years the organ had received no attention other than regular tuning and minor maintenance; a major overhaul was long overdue. At first he was disappointed with its sound but then he made a discovery, the movement had been

One visiting organist found the boy's pumping inadequate and in the middle of his organ solo said in a loud, deep voice, "A little more wind, please."

physically restricted. He removed the offending part and, in his words, "…the wind leaks ceased and the organ sang sweetly once again." He described it as not large but a very fine musical instrument. It was well built and thoroughly deserved a long awaited restoration and clean.

Members were asked to make a decision between the restoration of the pipe organ and the purchase of a new electric organ. Despite Mr Carter's obvious enthusiasm it was decided to adopt the latter option; it was installed in January 2003.

The decision not to restore the pipe organ was a disappointment to many people including Hilary Nankivell, the deputy organist, who had been involved with the organ for many years. Hilary sought permission from the Church Council to start fund-raising to meet the cost of refurbishment and was delighted to receive its approval. In October 2003, with the support of her family and a small group of friends, the pipe organ fund was launched. Llewellyn Doble made the first generous donation and before long contributions were being received from Church members and other local people. Various events helped to swell the fund and by October 2005 the staggering sum of £13,000 had been raised.

A steering group was formed to co-ordinate the receipt of quotations and to oversee the work. Tenders for the work were invited from a number of companies including Hele and Co who had built the organ back in 1872. After consideration by the Steering Committee it was the tender from Terry and Andrew Fearn of Honiton which was accepted, for approximately £14,000.

Hilary said that the Fearns were very cooperative and carried out the work with great sensitivity using only materials and techniques available to the original builders. The organ was stripped down, cleaned and restored with some of the work carried out on site and the remainder in their workshop at Honiton. At the same time the Dulciana was replaced and a few other alterations undertaken (this is included for the more technical readers:

The organ during its renovation 2006.

any queries should not be sent to the authors).

The organ was back in use for the carol service in December 2006 and the minister, Joan Watson, rededicated it in the following Easter Sunday morning service. A few weeks later Philip Davey, organist at Truro Methodist Church, and Clive Ellison, organist at St Agnes Parish Church, put it through its paces at a concert to celebrate the restoration. Sharing the concert was the Four Lanes Male Voice Choir under the inimitable Alastair Taylor. The organists and singers served up a feast of entertainment to produce what must have been one of the best concerts ever held in the Chapel. There was one touch of sadness however: Terry Fearn had died before the concert took place.

Hilary Nankivell had been the deputy organist since the mid 1950s. She had been encouraged and advised by Doris Ward and apart from a break for college, and when she married Pat Nankivell who whisked her away to Truro for a few years, she was on hand to cover for Ronnie Jeffrey, Ruth Jennings and Lyn Hewins. When Lyn retired in 2007 Hilary was appointed St Agnes Chapel Organist.

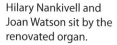

Hilary Nankivell and Joan Watson sit by the renovated organ.

The Choir
The choir had a long tradition of both leading the singing and of providing entertainment. It also seems to have been a powerful faction within Chapel life and to have ruffled a few feathers across the years.

Back in the 1870s the Trustees were faced with a crisis. The exact nature of the problem is not recorded but it was described as "serious." It caused them to pass a vote of confidence in the choirmaster and dissolve the choir. One man was so aggrieved at his dismissal that he protested until he was allowed to address the Trustees. It was finally resolved that he should be thanked for his past services and, in consideration of his long connection with the choir, he should be given a free sitting.

An attempt was then made to form a new choir by balloting the sacked male singers (perhaps a sort of divide and rule tactic). We wish that we could tell you how it was resolved but let's hope that it was an amicable solution. We can say that there is no record of any females being balloted. This may, of course, simply mean that the problem was restricted to the men or perhaps the women were not allowed to vote, even in this situation.

There were 27 members of the choir in 1900; we know that because their names were listed on the cover of William Tremewan's hymnbook. Many surnames are still associated with St Agnes.

Bass:
Frank Henwood (Goonbell)
Bert Harper (Higher Bal)
Fred Pope
George Henwood
John Osborne
William Tremewan (Goonvrea)
Ernest Rogers (Goonown)
Josiah Reynolds (Water Lane)
John Lawry (Goonown).

Alto:
Mary Ann Barkle (Goonown)
Maud Chapman (Higher Bal)
Jane Hooper
Clara Willcocks.

Soprano:
Bertha Willcocks
Winnie Hall
Beatrice Gribben (Quay)
Mary Henwood (Goonbell)
Ethel Rogers (Goonown)
Winnie Hill (possibly a
duplication)
Annie Hocking (Goonvrea)
Ethel Tremewan
(Goonvrea).

Tenor:
Fred Harper
John Hocking (Goonvrea)
Wm Henry Harper
(Higher Bal)
Archie Tremewan
(Goonvrea)
Charles Colenso Uren
(Goonvrea)
Tommy Harris.

In July 1902 the choir's annual outing was in Stribley and James' brakes to Mawgan Woods where they had their dinner. After enjoying a walk and viewing the convent and church they travelled to Newquay for tea. Then, after "traapzing" around the town, they left for home at 8.00pm where they arrived three hours later.

There was another problem in July 1907 when the Chapel Leaders were again faced with a mutinous choir. It was described as "a matter of great concern." The choir had announced its intention to resign en bloc after the next Sunday service. Once again, the meeting minutes do not describe the circumstances nor do they state if the threat was carried out but the Leaders talked of their deep regret and representatives were asked to plead with the choir that the action should be reconsidered or, at least, deferred.

The annual outing was a popular feature of choir life. It was a chance to gather socially with those who shared the task of leading the singing. Often it meant a trip to a coastal location and in July 1909 the members were off to Carbis Bay.

A brass quartet from Truro Band took part in the annual Wesleyan Choir Festival in March 1909; one young man who clearly made a good impression on his violin was Horace Cornish. Mrs Cornish and John Angwin shared the role of accompanist.

above; The Chapel
Choir in Falmouth on
the 1st July 1911.

top; The Chapel Choir
at Chapel Porth on the
14th July 1910.

Margaret Davey recalled the choir as particularly strong in her young days with 40 or 50 members attending a normal weekly service. She said that for special events a few people joined from other chapels and the number was even larger. She became a member when she was quite young, sometime around 1930, and recalled the singers gathering in the two rooms on either side of the organ. She said, "We all filed out and sat in the two rows of seats. It was an impressive sight, the large choir, the organ and the imposing rostrum with the large brass paraffin lamps on either side."

Music played a large part in chapel life. Cecil Langford was particularly busy: not only did he lead the choir but from 1928 he also conducted the St Agnes Silver Band. Local printer John Angwin also devoted a huge amount of time to the choir and to almost every other aspect of the Chapel. His daughter, Doris Ward, followed him as organist, a position she held for some time.

The Chapel could boast an excellent choir for many years. Colin Butson has a good memory of it and of the many people involved, particularly the Jennings family: Henry, Flo, Stanley (Rummy) and his wife, Ruth, who was also the organist. Other stalwarts who sprang to mind were the quartet of Freda Reynolds (soprano), Muriel Kneebone (contralto), Luther Stephens (tenor) and Frank Kneebone (bass).

A regular feature at Christmas was the rendition of "Ring the Bells," a carol by John Rogers. His great nephew, Malcolm Rogers, thinks that it was probably written in the early 1900s.

On Good Friday evening the choir always performed one of the shorter oratorios such as Stainer's "Crucifixion," Maunder's "Olivet to Calvary" or excerpts from the "Messiah". One year it was "Elijah" and on the 11th April 1948 a performance of Handel's oratorio "Samson" was hailed as outstanding. Miss Ivy M Johns, Mrs W J Shrimpton and Mr C J Borlase took the solo parts and were said to be excellent. The really musical ears in the audience had noticed a few dissonances in the performance but this was put down to an administrative problem; the organist's new copy of the music differed slightly from the soloists'.

The Revd Joe Ridholls recalled the choir in the late 1950s as large and influential in Chapel affairs. The Revd Philip Williams, from about ten years later, remembered its contribution as, "So much a part of the services." He said, "Whenever I finished a meeting at one of the other chapels early enough I called in at choir practice. On one occasion Frank Kneebone dropped his music as I came in and when he picked it up he turned to the wrong page. Miss Ivall, the Choirmistress, stopped the choir and said, 'What happened there, Mr Kneebone?' He replied, 'I'm sorry, Miss Ivall, the minister put me off.'"

The Rendering of the "Messiah" by the choir (Augmented) on January 21st 1952.

The deaths of Henry, Stanley and Flo Jennings and the move away of some other members depleted the choir, especially of men. Eventually the few remaining women left and it ceased to function as a choir.

The Manse

In 1886 the Revd William Heddon Major and the Trustees purchased a house in Vicarage Road at a cost of £270. It was to be the new Manse. Before that, other houses were used, one possibly in Rosemundy and another at the bottom of British Road, where Cleaderscroft now stands.

Professor Lamplough recalled the house in a letter he wrote in 1973 about his father, the Revd J Lamplough, the minister in 1890/91.

"The old granite Manse, as it is now called, reminded me of the fearful blizzard in 1891 when it began to snow one evening and in the night the snow drifted and piled up, covering the ground floor windows; they said that to telegraph to London one had to go via New York. My bedroom was at the back and I could see the red and white flashes of Padstow Lighthouse. We children did not go to school, my father instructed us at home and on our

The Manse c.1910.

walks to the beach, the beacon, mines etc. I was nine or ten when I had my first lessons in algebra.

Stephen Normanton, Lay Pastor at St Agnes 1986 - 1987 and his wife Phillippa.

We went to St Agnes by broad gauge train in 1890 and returned by narrow, ordinary gauge, in 1891. Free education came in at the same time. We had to fetch drinking water from a well, letting down buckets and carrying water in pitchers. I believe the pitchers were called fribbles."

The Manse was sold in 1986, exactly 100 years later. Mike Ashmore now lives there and kindly provided us with this information.

Stephen Normanton became the St Agnes Lay Pastor in 1986 and on the 28th August he moved into the new Manse at Castle Meadows which had been completely furnished for him. The Manse remained there for a few years, on land once owned by the Chapel, but in the mid 1990s it moved to Penwinnick Close where the present Minister, Joan Watson, lives.

The Chapel Tennis Court in the early 1920s.

The Tennis Court

Margaret Davey thinks that the Methodist Tennis Club at St Agnes started in the Revd Frank Poad's time as minister; this would have been in the early 1920s. The court was situated in the field below the Chapel entrance, where the terrace of three houses now stands. The open-fronted pavilion with its long seat at the front was an ideal place to watch the games. It was also popular for social gatherings and was well equipped with changing rooms at each end.

Margaret said, "The club had been running for a number of years before I joined; you had to be 16 years old before they would let you play. Clyde Pope and Russell Roberts were usually there and I remember Roy Blewett and Noel Hoskins playing when they could get away from their farm work. On one occasion I took part in a match against St Mary's Chapel in Truro. It was the last time I played with my husband, Horton. He had his own way of playing doubles and it certainly didn't suit me. After the home games we had our supper in the pavilion. The homemade food was laid out on a long table and a primus stove was used to boil the water. Lester Roberts played his ukulele and as we sang, passers-by often stopped to listen. We included all the favourite songs of the day and always finished with 'Moonlight and Roses.'"

During the Second World War some of the airmen from the military camp played tennis there and also attended some of the social events in the Chapel. But with so many men at war it became more and more difficult to find anyone to cut the grass and mark out the court so it was a case of war stopped play. The land was eventually sold and the houses built.

Ministers, Officers and Leaders

These Trustees, appointed in 1858, were responsible for building the new Chapel. The membership consisted entirely of men, a situation that prevailed until 1961.

James Rogers (Draper)
Thomas M Ninnis (Mine Agent)
John Hancock (Mine Agent)
Thomas Blenkinsop (Accountant)
Richard Davies (Mine Agent)
Edmund Penrose (Hatter)
Richard Rickard (Shoemaker)
Elisha Rowe (Shopkeeper)
Samuel Hooper (Miner)
Nicholas Bryant (General Agent)

John Evans (Founder)
John Peters (Farmer)
William Butson (Farmer)
Henry Peters (Miner)
Nicholas Langdon (Mason from Mingoose)
John Goyne Jnr (Accountant from Mount Hawke)
John Cock (Yeoman)
Sampson Stephens (Merchant from Penryn)
Thomas Mitchell (Miner from Perran)

Brothers T Stephens and H Peters were appointed Society Stewards in 1883 but in this time of hardship there was also the need for Poor Stewards; Brothers W Vivian and J Tremewan were elected to that position.

The United Meeting of Leaders, Stewards and Trustees was convened for a meeting on the 16th May 1883 for a matter which must have caused a good deal of concern. The members were to hear and decide on certain charges preferred by Frederick Nicholas, Richard Rickard and Thomas Stephens against Elisha Tregellas. We do not know the nature of the charges but the tone of the minutes suggests that they were substantial. Perhaps making use of the old adage that the best form of defence is attack, Elisha brought counter-charges against the same three gentlemen. The Revd R Daw presided over the meeting attended by 15 gentlemen including the plaintiffs who were, of course, also the defendants. The minutes state that after a full hearing of the various charges and examination of Robert Hancock, William Harris and George Williams Jnr as witnesses, Elisha Tregellas handed his resignation to the Chairman. Mr Daw and four other gentlemen met again on the 18th May to discuss the matter. The minutes record that after a free and long conversation it was decided not to take any further steps as Elisha Tregellas was no longer a member of the Wesleyan Methodist Society. It was unanimously agreed to dismiss the charges against the other three gentlemen. We are sorry to have whetted your appetite and raised your curiosity but we too are left to ponder at the nature of the charges which had resulted in such action.

The Revd Robert Daw, Wesleyan Minister at St Agnes 1872 - 1882.

At the Leaders' Meeting in January 1890 John Lawry Snr was appointed Leader in place of Brother James Rickard who, in the words of that period, was "just removed by death."

The Revd G W Thompson, the Minister at St Agnes for the past three years, preached his farewell sermon in August 1906. He was leaving the North Cornwall Mission and was presented with a magnificent testimonial in the form of a book. Under each of his various chapels is a list of subscribers; the pages are full of St Agnes parish names.

The Leaders' Meeting minute book of June 1913 referred to Brothers Solomon and Berryman holding open-air meetings at the Quay Meeting House. Perhaps their action caused some disquiet amongst the members but after some discussion it was resolved that they be allowed to continue their work.

The Revd G W Thompson, Wesleyan Minister at St Agnes 1903 - 1906.

The Revd Sylvester Lee,
Wesleyan Minister at
St Agnes 1912 - 1915.

The Revd Frank E Poad,
Wesleyan Minister at
St Agnes 1921 - 1923 with
the boys' class of 1923.

The Revd Harry Taylor, Wesleyan Minister at St Agnes 1923 - 1926.

In 1933 Mrs F G Gray, the Minister's wife, was elected President of the Women's Department; Mrs Gilpin the Treasurer and Miss A M Matthews the Magazine Secretary. Mr and Mrs Pengelly – he was the Station Master – left St Agnes in 1933 and a glowing tribute of their work was included in the Leaders' Meeting minutes. There was praise too for James Tredinnick who had completed 50 years service as a local preacher.

In 1937 John Angwin and Vic Trezise were re-elected as representatives to the Sunday school and Mr Redvers Bennetts was elected as a Society Steward. Unfortunately he subsequently had to decline due to work commitments.

An item in the "West Briton" in September 1947 referred to Miss Betty Tredinnick, a young local preacher on trial in the Perranporth and St Agnes Circuit, who had recently graduated from London University. For a while she stayed in London to work but in 1955 she returned. Betty's early connection with Methodism was at Mingoose where she began Sunday school in 1929, at the age of three. The family moved to Goonvrea in 1931 but she continued Sunday school and afternoon service at Mingoose and attended also St Agnes Methodist Chapel evening service until going to college in 1944. Her father, Eddie Tredinnick (1889 to 1983), became Senior Society Steward and Secretary to the St Agnes Methodist Trust for many years and was involved in Chapel activity up to the time of his death.

John Berryman, Cornwall County Councillor and local preacher, was involved in chapel life for many years. His wife, Emmie, was a sister of Eddie Tredinnick and their daughter, Christine, married Bill Morrison. In his book, "Jack Of All Trades," Bill Morrison wrote that you don't go to a Methodist chapel for long before you are asked to do something. He began his involvement at St Agnes Chapel by taking the collection. For a while he managed to avoid a larger involvement but then, in 1951, Betty Hocking gave him a shock by inviting him to become Sunday school Superintendent. It was only after considerable thought and discussion that he accepted. A few years later Bill began his preaching career but not before he had undergone an intensive period of study; the Revd Joe Ridholls tutored him and Roy Blewett and they were both accredited in 1961.

Glancing through the 1952 St Agnes Methodist Chapel Year Book and Directory we come across many familiar names in the list of officers, many no longer with us.

Society Stewards - W Pope, C Brokenshire, B Jones and J E Tredinnick.
Poor Stewards - V Trezise and C Pope
Class Leaders - A E Solomon, Mrs C Oates, Mrs W Pope and Miss C McDonald
Chapel Stewards - A E Solomon, C Pope and J Olds
Trust Secretary - J E Tredinnick
Trust Treasurer - A E Reynolds

> Recalling his younger days Eddie Tredinnick said that Sunday alternated between chapel attendance and farm chores, punctuated by constant changing from working clothes to best suit and back again.

Women's Work Fellowship Secretary - Miss C McDonald
Women's Work Fellowship Treasurer - Mrs J E Tredinnick
Guild Secretaries - J Thomas and H Hoare
Youth Club Secretary - J Thomas
Sunday school Secretary - Miss B Hocking
Choir Secretary - Mrs F Kneebone
Caretaker - R Richards

The arrival of a particularly charismatic young man in 1957 was to have a profound affect on the chapels at St Agnes and the surrounding villages. The Revd Joseph A D Ridholls had become the new Minister. Joe, as he became known, was responsible for eight chapels in the Perranporth and St Agnes Circuit: St Agnes, Beacon, Goonbell, Mingoose, Mithian, Mount Hawke, Silverwell and Trevellas and Crosscoombe. He had begun preaching at the age of 17 and in 1957 he moved from Derby to the Southwest. He was a Plymouthian by birth but with two Cornish grandmothers he could rightly claim to have come home.

In 1961 the membership of the Trust was reviewed and the changes could only be described as radical. For the first time the St Agnes Methodist Chapel Trust included ladies. The full list of those appointed were:

Alfred Ernest Solomon
Albert Edward Reynolds
Joseph Edwin Tredinnick
William Clyde Pope
Thomas Victor Trezise
Redvers Stephens Bennetts
John Berryman
William Roy Blewett
Nicholas Charles Thomas
Richard James Olds
Maxwell Hocking
Noel Hoskins

William Hume Morrison
Christine Emily Morrison
Agnes Butcher
Gertrude Margaret Davey
Mary Frances Oates
Elsie Irene Vanstone
Lester Roberts
Henry Russell Roberts
Roger Williams
Bessie Edwina Tredinnick
William Joseph Ronald Murrish

Christine Oates, the widow of the Headmaster of St Agnes School, lived in British Road and according to the Revd Joe Ridholls she referred to herself as a "twicer." This meant that she attended both the morning and evening service. She was stone deaf and usually asked the preacher before the service what the text or theme would be so that she could have it in mind. Joe said, "If she was unimpressed with the preacher she turned off her hearing aid." Another lady he recalled was Gladys Rogers who could quote Wesley's hymns by heart.

The Trustees in 1961.

In 1962 it was time for the Revd Joe Ridholls to move on and St Agnes said its goodbyes as he and Joan headed off to minister in the Cambridge Circuit. It was not the last that the parish would see of him.

The Circuit and Church Directory for 1977 provides us with a few more local names of people who have worked so hard for the local Methodist community:

Stewards - Bill Morrison, Betty Tredinnick and Sydney Knight
Treasurer - Sydney Knight
Church Council Secretary - Mrs Christine Morrison
Pastoral Visitor - Bill Cheshire
Property Secretary - Roger Williams
Organists - Mrs M Jepps and Mrs H Nankivell

The Revd Philip Williams came to St Agnes in 1969 and is still rather proud of Redvers Bennetts' newspaper headline, "Cornishman invited." He recalled that this was a period when people were still adjusting to the

The Revd Philip Williams, Methodist Minister at St Agnes 1969 - 1974.

remodelled building. During the services the sound of voices would drift up from the schoolroom and this seemed to disturb some people who asked if anything could be done. Philip said, "We can't do much about it. We must thank God that the children are here and so involved in church life."

Another aspect which he enjoyed was the Not-So-Young-Club. He visited it regularly and after he left the Circuit he often returned to take their Harvest Festival meeting and to auction the goods.

The dissolution of the Boards of Trustees and the setting up of Church Councils in 1977 resulted in the retirement of two stalwarts who together had served for approximately 55 years: Mr J E Tredinnick as Secretary and

The Revd Ken Sadler Methodist Minister at St Agnes 1974 - 1979.

The Revd Graham Caink, Methodist Minister at St Agnes 1979 - 1986.

Mr A E Reynolds who had been the Treasurer. Mr J R Bennetts became the new Secretary. When he eventually stood down Roger Williams took over the role.

In September 1979 members from Mount Hawke, Silverwell, Beacon, Goonbell, Trevellas and Crosscoombe and St Agnes Chapels gathered in the Methodist hall for an informal meeting to welcome their new minister, the Revd Graham Caink. He was the last minister to live in the Manse in Vicarage Road and the first to occupy the new one at 5 Castle Meadows where he lived until he left St Agnes in 1986.

In August 1980 the Revd Joe Ridholls renewed his connection with St Agnes when he arrived to take up his appointment as Superintendent Minister of the Newquay,

Perranporth and St Agnes Circuit. Although he was not the Minister directly responsible for St Agnes and its chapels they were once again under his broad wing.

Joint editors, Denise Rogers and Dinah Teagle published the first edition of the St Agnes Methodist Church newsletter in October 1984 with the intention that it would be a quarterly production. Each edition was full of news of all of the groups within the Chapel and in this first one there was a story by Claire Thorley (aged nine) entitled "My Summer Holiday."

The Revd Steven Emery-Wright, Methodist Minister at St Agnes 1987 - 1990.

During the John Wesley Celebration Service in 1985 the Revd Joe Ridholls presented Kath Knight with her 40-year Local Preacher's Certificate. Ten years later, in 1995, she received her 50-year certificate. Kath and her husband, Syd, had joined St Agnes Methodist Society when they retired to Cornwall in 1974. In 2003 she stood down after 58 years as a Local Preacher.

The February 1986 newsletter included a sad announcement, the death of Noel Hoskins of Silverwell. It was a great loss for St Agnes Methodist Church and for the community in general.

In 1987 an American arrived to take over as the St Agnes Minister. The Revd Joe Ridholls had invited Steven Emery over to discuss the position. He said, "It was a typical American greeting: he saw me and his first words were, 'Hi Joe.'"

The "West Briton Argus" of February 1988 wrote, "Steven Emery runs through the village in his shorts, enjoys a tot or two of rum, can't sing a note, walks a pet rabbit instead of a dog and likes few things better than a good water-fight with the kids." It perhaps explains why he was such an immediate hit with the youth groups and why their numbers rose so dramatically during his stay.

The Revd Joe Ridholls in 2010.

The Revd J A D Ridholls retired as the Superintendent Methodist Minister of Newquay, Perranporth and St Agnes in 1989. At a farewell supper at St Agnes Jenny Osborne presented him with a cheque and Dinah Teagle gave his wife, Joan, a bouquet of flowers. They moved to Probus from where he continued to work part-time at Plymouth and in Truro, but the lure of St Agnes life proved strong and in 1994 they returned to live in the village. He recalled a telephone call from an elderly lady who told him that things weren't the same since he retired. She said, "They got dancin' down the Chapel now…twadn exactly decent. It's not so much what they're wearing, it's what they wad'n wearin.'"

The Revd Steven Emery married during his incumbency and he and his wife combined their names to become Mr and Mrs Emery-Wright. The October 1990 newsletter recorded the news of the baptism of their daughter, Hannah Sarah Emery-Wright, born that May.

In the same year Denis Bray of St Agnes celebrated 50 years as a local preacher. He had taken his first service in his home town of Helston and since then had preached in innumerable chapels across Cornwall and beyond. It was around this time that Margaret Hoskins retired from the Church Council, the body responsible for the day-to-day running of Chapel activities.

All good things come to an end and in July 1990 it was time for Steven Emery-Wright to take his leave. With his wife Lorraine and daughter Hannah he said his goodbyes and prepared for the journey from St Agnes to Michigan. His three-year period had clearly been a great success and he is still talked of with a lot of affection. His replacement, John Haley, arrived from Mitcham, Surrey, with his family and the Methodists at St Agnes prepared to get to know yet another new minister.

A report in the July 1991 newsletter stated, "As many of us know, Betty Tredinnick is off to the United States in August – yet again! But this time the main reason for going is to speak at a Retreat in Pennsylvania about the

The Revd John M Haley,
Methodist Minister at
St Agnes 1990 - 1994.

work of a British Local Preacher as that role no longer exists in the American Methodist Church. The folk leading the Retreat are the Revd and Mrs Russell Perry who were over here two years ago when Russell preached at Mount Hawke and St Agnes." When Betty returned she wrote about her 11,000-mile journey and the week she'd spent with the Emery-Wrights. She brought back their best wishes and said, "Hannah is growing apace and learning new words each day; she is a real charmer with a broad grin just like her Dad."

A new minister was welcomed to the Circuit in 1994, Cornishman the Revd Gerald Wallis, a man who was to leave a lasting legacy.

Ruth Jennings retired in 1997. She had been organist at St Agnes and other chapels in the area for 60 years and to mark the achievement the Methodist Music Society awarded her a Long Service Certificate. She began her

Ruth Jennings playing the St Agnes Chapel organ.

music career at Crosscoombe Primitive Chapel and when that closed at the beginning of the Second World War she played at the old Trevellas Downs Chapel. From there it was a short move to the new Trevellas and Crosscoombe Chapel where she played until its closure. She was largely self-taught and her contribution was not limited to the organ as she also sang and helped to arrange many events. She was renowned for organising the Merritt carol and Sankey hymn evenings, something she had done on so many occasions at her original Chapel. When she died she was sadly missed for many years and still is.

The Revd Beverly Hollings arrived in the parish in September 1999 and took her first service lying down – literally. She was awaiting surgery for a back injury and could not stand for long so she lay on her front for most of the service. St Agnes was her first ministerial appointment since leaving theological college; her previous career was as a teacher.

The Revd Beverly Hollings, Methodist Minister at St Agnes 1999 - 2005.

Beverly Hollings (Bev the Rev as she called herself) took her leave in 2005 to become District Evangelism Enabler in Yorkshire. St Agnes then welcomed Martha Wedel Caputo from America who arrived to spend a year in St Agnes on the British-American Ministry Programme. Martha clearly enjoyed her time in the village and described Cornwall as the source of her Methodist roots.

Writing in the Spring/Summer 2006 edition of "In Touch" the Revd Nigel Deller, Superintendent Minister, used the heading of "Chapel or Church?" for his lead article. It seems that his "upcountry" ministerial friends had become a little irritated when he talked of Methodist chapels rather than Methodist churches. The article pans out into an observation about underused chapel buildings but it is interesting that this should have surfaced at a time when we were grappling with which to use. We were discussing this with the Revd Joe Ridholls who seemed quite unconcerned about it and agreed that it was traditionally a case of Anglicans and their church and Methodists with their chapel.

Undoubtedly the building itself was always referred to as a chapel; however, there are clearly many, in Cornwall at least, who would still ask if you are church or chapel to distinguish between Anglicans and Methodists.

In September 2006 the Revd Joan Watson, a Penzance girl, arrived to take care of this part of the Circuit. Clearly proud of her Cornish heritage, Joan was delighted to tell us that the Communion at the St Agnes Synod in spring 2009 was conducted in Kernewek (the Cornish Language). The Revd Julyan Drew of Penzance, Cornish linguist and a friend from her school days, took the service.

The Revd Joe Ridholls came out with one of his wry quotations from an old member, "Tid'n hardly nobody never go nowhere."

Events

There is occasional reference to temperance in St Agnes and while we are not too sure of the official line in the early days, in 1883 there was a decision, which still remains, to use non-intoxicating wine for future sacramental services.

In his book, "How to get methodical with your Cornish Methodists," the Revd Colin Short makes it clear that Methodism was not a teetotal movement. Indeed, we have found reference to early preachers being provided with refreshment comprising bread and beer. But many people considered alcohol to be damaging to family life and there were Temperance Sunday collections. In 1925, for example, the money raised was allocated to the St Agnes Band of Hope.

Also in the 1883 meeting it was agreed that a special service would be held on future Feast Days, the nearest Monday to the 21st January.

Every celebration of note warranted a tea and this was the case for the new converts at Goonown Schoolroom in March 1891. It was free but there were boxes available just in case anyone felt like making an offering. There was a tea on Boxing Day in 1902 when a 100 people attended and paid 6d each but the smaller children who took part in the afternoon entertainment received theirs free. The festive celebration was rounded off with an evening oratorio. A Foreign Missionary deputation visited the village in March 1903. It was clearly an important event and Doctor Whitworth and Mr J Tremewan were given the job of providing hospitality. Such provision was normal in Methodist circles and the preachers' accommodation plan indicated the name of the person responsible for providing meals for the visiting preacher each Sunday.

Even in April 1909 the topic for the Men's Meeting probably caused a few smiles, particularly among the ladies invited as guests. The Revd William Rider posed the question, "Is a man too old at forty?" It did not define the purpose behind the question and it would be a brave person who suggested it today unless, of course, it was with humorous intent. To conclude the evening Mr Alfred Solomon provided a cornet solo and John Angwin conducted the Male Voice Choir.

It must have been with a mixture of sadness and pride that this huge crowd gathered in the Chapel grounds on the 14th February 1920 to witness the unveiling of the new war memorial. It was very unusual for one to be located in the grounds of a Methodist chapel but in St Agnes there was no room by the Parish Church.

UNVAILING OF WAR MEMORIAL ST. AGNES.   FEB. 14. 1920.

A request which may seem unusual in these days appeared at least a couple of times in the minute books. It was for a service in aid of the Society for the Propagation of the Gospel among the Jews. It was granted and one was held in January 1910.

On Monday the 15th March 1926 St Agnes celebrated the visit of the Revd John H Ritson, President of the Conference. The souvenir programme contained advertisements for a great number of local businesses and we felt it interesting to include them.

W H Cowl - Baker and Confectioner in Churchtown
J Reynolds and Son - Painters etc in Vicarage Road
T E Dunstan - Chemist
W H Newton - Engineer in Peterville
W Tonkin - Provision Merchant in Churchtown
E M Uglow - Tailor and Outfitter
A L Harris - Butcher in Churchtown
J Letcher - Grocer in Peterville
S H Richards - Greengrocer
F J and E L Gribben - Ladies' and Gents' Hairdresser of Vicarage Road
J H Vellenoweth - Butcher in Churchtown
A I Reynolds - Grocer
T J Delbridge - Footwear, Ironmongery, Car hire, Vehicle components and Travel Booking Agent of Fore Street, St Agnes (note the reference to Fore Street)

The Revd John Ritson took the service followed by, of course, a tea. Holders of blue meal tickets had to go to the Oddfellows Hall (now the Meadery) while those with red tickets were fed in the Vestry.

Margaret Davey recalled Christmas time, Easter and other occasions when there were so many in the congregation that they had to sit in the aisles. She said, "For the harvest celebrations, sheaves of wheat, oats and barley were taken into the back vestry and sorted into small bunches. They were tied up with fine string; it took ages but we enjoyed the work. Mrs Mildred Roberts then arranged them in wonderful patterns on the carved rails of the rostrum."

St Agnes man, Alderman W J Kemp, became Mayor of Truro in 1942. In honour of this local man and in appreciation of the reflected honour for St Agnes, John King of Mithian, Chairman of Truro Rural District Council, arranged the Civic Service at St Agnes Chapel.

The St Agnes Methodist News Bulletin of June 1947 wrote of a double celebration on the 6th July 1947: the 85th anniversary of the opening of the Chapel for public worship and the 200th anniversary of the first visit of the Revd John Wesley to St Agnes. It was interesting to find a reference to "Big Chapel" in the October 1947 News Bulletin. Perhaps this nickname has been largely forgotten but in that year, and possibly for some time before, it was in regular use.

The Methodist News Bulletin of Perranporth and St Agnes Circuit in May 1948 talked of a "splendid beginning" as more and more young people were dedicating their lives to Christ. Seventeen from Perranporth and eight or nine from Goonhavern were said to be the first fruits of a growing youth movement. Many had attended the Circuit Youth Rally at Perranporth chaired by Noel Hoskins and addressed by the Revd Fred Hickling.

Margaret Davey spoke of the Trustees being all-powerful. She said, "They took care of the building and worked hard to keep it in good repair. Of course, the ladies also did their share; they provided food for every occasion, all home-baked. It was given, so every penny raised was for the Chapel. The items for the bazaars and sales, like pillowcases, cushion covers, bed-jackets and socks, took months to make. A lot of it was beautifully embroidered; it represented hours of work but it raised the money to keep the Chapel solvent."

Even today, at Coffee Mornings, the cake stall is one of the most popular and there are many who can knock up a cake or a sponge good enough to entice a man to the altar! Back in 1933 the ladies of St Agnes Methodist Church decided to record their culinary knowledge in a recipe book with more mouth-watering treats than you can imagine including, of course, the Cornish pasty and saffron cake. Many years later, Hilary Nankivell produced a similar book entitled "Tried and Tested."

The Revd Joe Ridholls shared a story with us which must have caused a little embarrassment: Eddie Tredinnick was trying to contact Henry Gribben to ask if he would take the Sunday service at St Agnes Chapel. He happened to be at the Epiphany Home where Henry's son worked so he said to him, "Do me a favour, Tony, ask father if he'll take the service next week." Now there was a young Anglican curate there, the chaplain to the sisters whom they referred to as "Father." Tony must have thought it a bit strange but he went to the curate and passed on the invitation. Luckily the mistake was realised in time and the arrangements unscrambled.

The Revd Joe Ridholls was unhappy with some of the Revd Dr Donald Soper's remarks about Billy Graham's campaign. He said, "I criticised him and challenged him to bring the Order of Christian Witness (O C W) to St Agnes. To his credit he accepted and in September 1959 he arrived."

Dr Soper took part in an "Any Questions" session at the Cameron Estate meeting house and spoke during the interval at the Regal Cinema. The Revd Joe Ridholls said, "He came to our house where he met some of the girls from the Rosemundy Home for unmarried mothers. He preached in the Chapel and made a great impression." Events were held in the chapels at St Agnes, Trevellas, Goonbell, Beacon and Cameron Estate with open-air forums at St Agnes Square and at the beach. The final rally of the week's campaign was held in St Agnes Chapel; it was one of the largest attended services of Holy Communion ever held there. Dr Soper was the principal speaker and appealed to three sections of the

St Agnes Methodist Church once featured on BBC Radio. A service broadcast in March 1952 was recorded there and for a short while put St Agnes on the broadcasting map. Richie Sandercock remembered the occasion, he said, "The Revd Frank White came over well, his voice was particularly suited to radio."

The cover of the order of service from the BBC broadcast.

community: those inside the church, those on the fringe and those completely outside. Mr W J Sheaff, formerly of St Agnes and leader of the O C W campaign team, spoke of the need to weave Christianity into the whole fabric of life.

St Agnes Methodist Chapel was almost filled for the two services to celebrate the 112th anniversary in July 1974 when the, by then, Revd the Lord Soper, former President of the Methodist Conference, conducted the services and was delighted to renew his friendship with the members at St Agnes. Brian Roberts recalled him being referred to as "the Lord" and when Bill Morrison gave him a lift through the village Brian's young son, Matthew, exclaimed, "Dad, there's the Lord in a camper van."

Lord Soper came again in 1994, 95, 96 and 97. He preached in the Chapel on the first two occasions but after that was too crippled with arthritis to mount the stairs. In 1997 he presented Betty Tredinnick with her 50-year certificate as a Local Preacher during his service at Crantock.

The 200th anniversary of John Wesley's last visit to St Agnes was as good a reason as any for a celebration and as he last came to the village in 1785 we guess that the undated programme of events relates to 1985. It included a series of Slide Shows by Bill Morrison entitled "A Passel of Old Traade," "St Agnes Past and Present," "The Changing Scene" and "A Tribute to the G W R." There was also a Cornish Evening and, on the 28th August, the actual celebration of Wesley's last visit. The Revd Joe Ridholls took the service and preached the same text used by Wesley 200 years before.

The 1985 newsletters not only included the 200th Wesley anniversary, they also reported the 125th anniversary of the Chapel building (laying of foundation stone) and some spectacular success at the Circuit Youth Day "It's a Knockout" competition held at Goonhavern. The youth teams did well but it was the adult team which

Revd the Lord Soper during one of his later visits to St Agnes.

triumphed. Having reluctantly entered they surprised everyone by winning their final. The report seems to show a particularly poor display of confidence in the team who came away with the shining trophy but, for the sake of history, the victorious team comprised Pam Williams, David Teagle, Brian Roberts, Nigel Oates and Bill Cheshire.

In the April 1988 Newsletter John Briney urged people to take part in the 250th anniversary of Wesley's conversion. He asked them to join in the Wesley Celebration Parade at the Victorian Fayre. A few years later, in 1997, St Agnes celebrated the 250th anniversary of Wesley's first visit to Cornwall. The event was a festival of flowers and eight Chapel windows were decorated with paintings and flowers depicting some of the places that he visited.

In an earlier chapter we referred to the divisions within the churches but in St Agnes there are now positive signs of closer relationships. One example was on the 25th April 1999, under the heading of "Churches Together in St Agnes" when the Anglican, Catholic and Methodist churches combined for their service.

The Building – Additions and Alterations

A new rostrum and communion rail was installed in 1882 and we can only speculate on what had previously been used. In many chapels the preacher would have stood at a simple lectern, probably on a raised platform.

In 1901 a new vestry was needed and Mr Sampson Hill was asked to undertake the design; his fee was £5.5s. Following completion of the work the Revd Hudson Smith performed the opening ceremony. The inevitable public tea followed.

By 1909 the heating and lighting was becoming a bit dated and it was decided that it needed to be replaced. According to the "Royal Cornwall Gazette" the cost of the work would be about £300. The money was found and the work carried out. To celebrate the new installation

The new rostrum and communion rail which was installed in 1882 decorated for harvest.

Mr James Wickett presided at a public lunch. Mrs Hodson Smith and Mrs R Waters performed what was referred to as the "door-opening ceremony;" Mr H C Tonking of Newquay gave an organ recital and Miss Elsie Williams played a violin solo.

Convenience lighting arrived in 1928 when electricity replaced the old petrol and gas system. A payment to the West Cornwall Electricity Supply Co Ltd for the installation of lights and fixtures appears in the accounts but it was a return to oil lighting in October 1929 when the lights went out; the new technology had failed. For a while it seemed that there would be an early conclusion to the service but the sermon was saved when the lights flickered on just in time.

Mr Henry Letcher made "periodic" repairs to the Chapel timepiece and in 1922 Mr M Hodge was paid £69 for new seats. Charles Chegwin, builder and St Agnes bandsman, carried out various items of repair work to the Chapel and in 1926 he built a ladies' toilet; Mr Orchard undertook the plumbing. In the same year Mr H Hodge carried out the work for the choir loft rearrangement.

In 1948 the Trustees discussed essential repairs and adaptations to the building to make it more suitable for Sunday school use. They warned that the proposed work would be expensive and that everyone would be required to help. The Youth Guild was doing its bit by organising a fete and sports.

According to the "News-notes of The Methodist Church for St Agnes and Mount Hawke" the Chapel premises were a bit shabby in 1951. The Trustees were anxious to make them bright, attractive and welcoming but it was the age-old problem, a shortage of money. A special appeal was made for gifts to cover the cost which was estimated at £300. It doesn't seem much now but sixty years ago it was a huge sum.

By the mid 1980s the exterior of the building was beginning to look a bit dowdy again and in need of a facelift. Lawrence Fox, Property Secretary, hoped that roof repairs and redecoration work would start soon and that a public address system would be installed: £5,000 was needed to cover the cost.

By 2009 the kitchen facilities were proving inadequate for current needs, particularly for the twice-monthly cooked meals prepared for the elderly folk of the parish. A new kitchen to modern standards was needed. It was formed within the existing hall, on the north side in a space partly occupied by a store. The old kitchen servery on the other side of the room was removed so the loss of usable floor space was minimal. The cost, including all the equipment, was about £40,000.

Back in 1967 Mrs Nancy Homer, a well-known art teacher and potter living in "Wayside Cottage," was asked to paint a mural for St Agnes Primary School. She did so with the help of another art teacher, Mrs Phyllis Chubb. It was an amalgam of typical Cornish village buildings and countryside. When the new school opened there was no room for it and it spent the next four years in storage. In 1992 it was given to the Methodists and erected in the Chapel Hall where it still adorns the front wall.

The 1964 Project

In 1964 work began on the extensive project to floor in the gallery, but the story does not start there as the ground had been well and truly prepared over a great number of years.

At the Annual Trustee Meeting in January 1943 a controversial idea was floated: John Angwin asked if consideration could be given to carrying out alterations to the Chapel in order that the congregation could be seated on one level. A sub-committee was formed with the remit to investigate the possibility of converting the gallery into the Chapel and using the ground floor as a schoolroom. The committee comprised the Revd W N Warren, J R S Bennetts, R Waters, A E Reynolds, J E Tredinnick and John Angwin.

The idea was developed over the next few years but, as ever, funding was a problem. An alternative proposal that the Sunday school could use a Nissen hut in the Chapel fields was not considered feasible and was rejected. It was stalemate and the idea was tucked away but not forgotten.

Bill Morrison reflected on the size of congregations in 1950 when there could be 60 at the morning service and 200 in the evening. The Chapel was one of the largest and most active organisations in the village, it was central to community life. Within a few years however, numbers began to fall and Bill referred to the smaller numbers spread out across a Chapel designed for 960.

For many, the single floor Chapel was the answer and in September 1952 it again came to the fore. Funding was still a problem but the Trustees felt that it was important to find out how everyone felt about the scheme in principle. It was agreed to canvass the views of the congregation. Bill Morrison wrote that many opposed the idea and that when the votes were counted those against had won the day. He recalled one old lady with a particular concern who said, "They'll end up having pantomimes in the hall – heaven above and hell below."

previous page; The pulpit and organ before alterations in 1964.

It was a setback but the vote was not the end of the matter. Back in 1936, Richard Waters (Captain Dick Waters or Cap'n Dick) had donated £600 to floor in the gallery. He could foresee that the 960-seater building would be much too large for future needs. He must have been very shrewd because he included a caveat that the money should not be used for any other purpose than that stipulated, viz. to floor in the gallery. If the Trustees wanted the money they had to comply exactly with his wishes.

According to Bill Morrison, the Sunday school Council in 1955 pleaded that new or altered premises were urgently needed. The Trustees called a meeting of interested parties to discuss possible solutions. For some, the division of the Chapel was a step too far. There was horror at the idea of scrapping the large pulpit and many felt it was wrong that people would be forced to climb the stairs to worship. Mr Tredinnick explained that it would be an easy stair, each step would only have a small rise. Matt Radcliffe was not to be swayed and said that he supposed it would be so easy that it would be like going downhill. For one reason or another the proposal was rejected once again.

By now the traditionalists in the congregation must have wondered what they had to do to defeat the proposal as in spite of this recent rejection, the scheme for a first floor Chapel was still on the table and continued to appear on meeting agendas. Clearly the idea was not going to go away and when it was raised again, Mr A E Reynolds, Mr W C Pope, Mr L Roberts and Mr J E Tredinnick were tasked with investigating the likely cost.

By 1960 no progress had been made on the major scheme but a smaller project was underway: a new kitchen was formed in the north vestry. For many, however, the creation of a single-level Chapel with schoolroom underneath was the ultimate aim.

In 1961, during the Revd Joe Ridholls' incumbency, the Trust signalled its intent as it appointed a new committee to pursue the single floor Chapel. It consisted of Mrs M Davey, Miss E Vanstone, Mr W H Morrison, Mr N Hoskins,

Mr R Murrish, Mr A E Reynolds and Mr J E Tredinnick: they set to work.

In 1962 the Revd Raymond Foster took over the reins at St Agnes and inherited the plan for the building alterations. There was renewed impetus amongst the Trustees and according to the minutes, three schemes emerged:

1. To floor in the well of the gallery.
2. To remove the gallery and build a new first floor.
3. To erect a new building with two vestries.

The second scheme was the preferred option but it was ruled out because of the cost. After considerable discussion the first option finally emerged as favourite. The building would be divided horizontally with a ground floor hall, vestries, kitchen and toilets and a first floor Chapel to seat 350 people – Cap'n Dick's caveat had won the day. Tony Gribben was asked to prepare some sketch plans for Mr K E Rundle of Cowell, Drewitt and Wheatley of Truro who was appointed architect.

Bill Morrison wrote, "Raymond Foster steered the Trustees through many meetings and problems after the architect's first plans. The heating system was an afterthought and had to be considered later, when people found that they were not warm enough. The provision of one toilet was considered inadequate despite it being continually referred to by the architect as 'the toilets.' The design of the front area raised some objections with the pulpit placed to one side in a Society where preaching was central, an altar for the Eucharist instead of a table for the Lord's Supper and a heavy communion rail that seemed to fence off the leaders from the people in what is essentially a lay church. But the architect won the day, as architects often do, by warning that the work would not be finished in time for the opening ceremony if any alterations were made. The Trustees did have the last word on one point, the colour of the organ pipes. Mr Rundle had wanted lime green but they insisted on shocking pink, or so some people called it, although the colour chart said terra cotta. The total cost in 1964 was £7,578, an astronomical amount. But we went ahead."

The farm and garden where Castle Meadows now stands was sold and added to the money already set aside. The Trustees pledged to raise a further £1,000 and the various sections of the Chapel also had their targets. Unfortunately Dick Waters' original £600 had been invested in a safe Government stock and was now worth only £400. Despite this reduction in value his contribution had ensured that his scheme was adopted but, according to Bill Morrison, some felt that the opportunity for a more drastic change was missed.

The Vicar and members of St Agnes Anglican Church kindly gave permission for services to be held in the Church Hall while the work was carried out and in January 1964 the Sunday school dispersed to various private houses. The Revd B A R Morris conducted the last service in the two-floor Chapel and the artefacts were hurriedly removed to make way for the contractors. It was a major project and it was hoped that work would proceed more smoothly than back in the 1860s when the Chapel was built.

St Agnes builder W H Waters was awarded the contract and in January 1964 he and his team arrived to begin the work. A number of local men were involved including Tony Gribben (Foreman), Jimmy Olds (Foreman Carpenter), Ralph Fowler, Henry Gribben, Gerald Bennallack and Irwin Roberts. Bill Waters had worked for Eddie Tredinnick for some years and was, no doubt, grateful for any input that he could provide throughout the contract. Percy James and David Doble undertook the electrical work and Hooper and Son of Truro the heating installation.

Bill Morrison was eager to record the progress of the work with his camera but he later wrote that he was asked to leave when they began erecting the large steel

---

Jimmy Olds was "full of fun" and never missed an opportunity to bring a smile to someone's face. Perhaps, however, that was not Russell Richards' reaction when he emptied the contents of the sack of offcuts that Jimmy had kindly given him. Old timbers made lovely burning wood and Russell must have thought that he had a "brave old load" when he picked it up. The few pieces at the top burned well but the stones below did not.

beams as the men felt unable to swear with him there.

The late delivery of the joinery from John Williams of St Austell caused a headache but the new pulpit, communion rail and table arrived in the nick of time – one day before the opening. The pulpit had been given in memory of James and Emily Tredinnick of Mingoose and Elsie Tredinnick. Albert Reynolds did a tremendous amount of work for the Chapel over the years and it was thanks to his generosity that the ground floor worship centre was furnished. Donations for the new Chapel were received from Mrs Sylvester Lee, the widow of a former minister, who gave the cross on the communion table, the Ball family in whose memory the carpet in the communion area was presented, the Women's Fellowship who gave the flower vases in the windows, Mrs Kathleen Johnson presented the pulpit copy of the New English Bible in memory of her husband and the Communion

Dismantling of the Chapel for the 1964 project.

Table was given by the Angwin family. The Communion Table in the Worship Centre was given in memory of Miss C MacDonald and, much later, a lectern in memory of Eddie Tredinnick was subsequently used in the Chapel.

The "free seats" from the sides of the old Chapel were to be re-used in the centre but they had previously been set against a wall and whereas one end was ornately carved, the other was not. Jimmy Olds set to with his chisels and glasspaper and did a superb job of replicating the carving on the blank ends. When these were replaced with chairs in the late 1990s a few were retained for use downstairs but most were sold. The pews in the original balcony were retained and are still in place but the pew doors were later removed to aid escape in the event of a fire. Health and Safety regulations did not exist when the pews were originally installed in the 1860s. Betty Tredinnick recalled that the new colour scheme was not immediately appreciated. She liked it but that was not

Looking up through the wood beams between the girders.

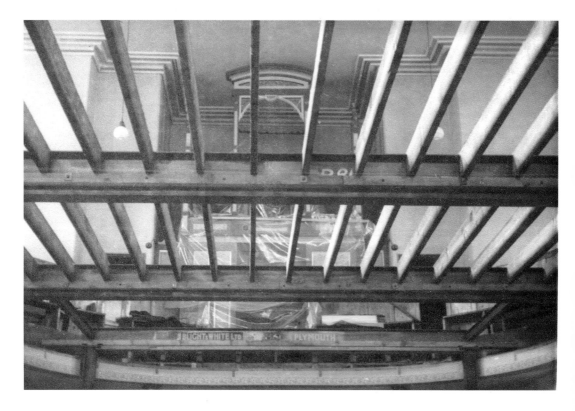

Jimmy Olds, Ralph Fowler and Tony Gribben lay the new wooden floor.

Floor polished, organ pipes in place and lights fitted.

The finished Chapel with centre pews in place.

too surprising as it was her suggestion. Finally, with the alterations complete and the hard work behind them, the members looked forward to the opening of their reconstructed Chapel.

On Friday the 5th June 1964, after a hymn and a prayer, Mrs H E Penter of Redruth formally opened the Richard Waters Memorial Chapel on the ground floor and the Revd F J B Quine offered a prayer of dedication. A little later Mrs C S Ward of St Agnes cut the white ribbon across

the entrance to the new hall and reconstructed Chapel and it was the turn of the resident Minister, Raymond Foster, to provide the prayer of dedication.

Following the formalities the congregation took its place in the Chapel for the service of dedication during which the Revd Dr Donald Soper preached the sermon. He referred to the superb appearance of the reconstructed Chapel and reflected on their Methodist ancestors who had been suspicious of beautiful things with the result that early chapels had looked rather more like barns than places of worship. A meeting of thanksgiving was held in the evening when Mr John Berryman took the chair and the Revd Dr Donald Soper and the Revd Hubert Luke, Chairman of the Methodist District, were the speakers. Mr J H Jennings led the choir in community hymn-singing. The following day, Saturday the 6th June, the Climax Male Voice Choir under Mr E S Kessell provided a concert chaired by Mr W J Kemp of Truro. The celebrations were concluded on the Sunday with a series of services.

Margaret Davey recalled that not everyone had been in favour of the alterations. Some preferred the layout as

The formal opening of the Richard Waters Memorial Chapel. l-r; Mr E Tredinnick, Revd F J Bushy Quine, Mr K E Rundle (The Architect), Mrs Doris Ward, Mrs H E Penter, Revd Hubert Luke, Revd Dr Donald Soper, Revd Raymond Foster and Mr W H (Bill) Waters (builder).

Sunday School children parade to the service in the new Chapel. *l-r;* Paul Renfree, ?, Gary Prisk, ?, ?, ?, Ann Claydon, Clive Benney, Brian Roberts, Richard Bamber, Roderick Mitchell and Neil Roberts.

l-r; Belinda Chapman, Tina Fabray, Jano Redfern, ?, June Lovering, ?, Sally Blewett, Jeanette Bawden, Elsie Vanstone, Stella Claydon, ?, Glynis Olds, Michael Bunt, Robert Prisk, Lesley Hoskins, Andrew Blewett, Bernard Hoskins, David Olds, Joy Waters, Ribena Hydman, Helen Hydman, Susan Murrish, Janet Olds, David Murrish, David Murrish (Mingoose), Malcolm Carveth, Stephen Bunt, ?

it was while others were simply against change of any sort. Now that it had been completed, however, it was clear that having the Chapel separate from the large ground floor hall opened up new opportunities, like the flower festivals with their beautiful pieces assembled by the members of the Floral Art Club, the Victorian exhibition with a spinning wheel, a gypsy evening with all the ladies in Romany dress and many other events. But the greatest benefit of all was that the youth groups had space to develop.

As with any new building the new layout was strange at first but within a short while the strange was transformed into the familiar.

The 1998 Project

Some of the well-founded doubts raised by those opposed to the major alteration of 1964 had proved to be correct: the stairs to the first floor Chapel had presented problems, for the disabled, the elderly and for coffin bearers. There were many who thought it undignified that coffins had to be lifted through a window and onto a half-landing before being carried up the final flight of stairs, though local undertakers managed it smoothly.

When the Revd Gerald Wallis became Minister in 1994 he strongly supported a scheme for a programme of improvements including the installation of a lift. It was extended to include re-slating the main roof, providing a better foyer, better toilets and a new kitchen. The balcony seating was to be retained but the old pews in the central area were to be replaced with comfortable individual chairs. A brochure was produced for the scheme, and although the ground floor layout ultimately differed from it the finished arrangement was a good solution. Fund raising began in February 1997 with a full week of events and the money raised added to that received from grants. The final cost was £365,000 and within one year of completion all monies had been raised or promised (by means of covenants). The work could proceed.

Ralph Fowler has many memories of the work being carried out including Irwin Roberts painting the high fascias off a ladder and of using roof timbers as scaffolding for the high ceiling. Ralph said, "There were two accidents that I can remember. David Doble put his foot through the moulded ceiling rose in the chapel and I managed to trip and fall on a protruding 4" nail which went straight through my hand."

l-r; The Revd Gerald Wallis, Barry Austin, Glynis Teagle, Ros Parker, Janet Cormack, Marilyn Shears, Doreen Ritchie, Derek Skinner, The Revd Dr Stephen Dawes (Chairman of the District).

Barry Austin was Chairman of the Development Committee. Andrew Buck of the Lilly Lewarne Partnership undertook the Architectural work, Michael Crook was the Consultant Engineer and John Cormack of St Agnes the Structural Engineer. In June 1998 the building contract was signed with E Thomas of Ponsanooth and work began.

While it was being carried out the services were held in the St Agnes Scout Hut but not for long as the work progressed smoothly and by early December it was complete. The congregation gathered for the re-opening service on the 24th January 1999. Gerald Wallis conducted the morning service and the Revd Dr Stephen B Dawes, Chairman of the District, re-dedicated the Chapel and preached the sermon. The celebration concert was held on the following Sunday when Treverva Male Voice Choir, soloist Emma Williams, St Agnes Silver

Band and John Hitchens, British euphonium Champion, provided the entertainment.

Sadly, Gerald Wallis did not live long enough to enjoy the fruits of his labour as he died just four months later, a few weeks before he was due to retire.

Financial Matters

The accounts book from 1899 to 1933 includes many items which illustrate the marked difference in chapel life from that time to this. Income came from such items as pew rent and from the collections, or "offerings" as one preacher insisted on calling them. These were regular and very necessary to cover the running costs.

Evidence that the Chapel owned an area of land greater than held today was the regular income for rent of farm to Mr G H Roberts, rent of garden to Captain Hooper, rent of field to G H Hancock and, intriguingly, rent of hedge to Thomas Martin for one penny per year. In January 1912 Mr C Harris provided coal at one shilling and four-pence per cwt and Charlie James sold paraffin at nine pence per gallon. In 1915 Mr H Stribley charged eight pence for one pound of lard for a machine (no doubt that will make sense to somebody). The preachers' horse had to be looked after and in 1899 a payment was made to James Gillard at Paull's Hotel for its stabling: in 1911 it cost one shilling and sixpence per day and the collection from a particular Sunday in February was in aid of the Horse Hire Fund.

Funds were not always readily available for items of special expenditure and it was quite usual for the Trustees to seek personal loans from within the membership. There were always those who were prepared and able to lend money to the Chapel and the accounts include quite a number of entries for interest paid. Collections were not restricted to Chapel services, they were also taken in the Sunday school, for the Sunday school itself, for the Methodist Homes for the Aged and the Junior Missionary Association (JMA) where the money was used for overseas work. Margaret Hoskins said that the children also collected money around the community for JMA and earned badges for their efforts. Such collections encouraged the children to give, not only for their own benefit but to help other people and those overseas in poor countries.

In June 1986 David Teagle, the Chapel Treasurer, was appealing for funds for a new heating system. With memories of the long cold spell the previous winter, and fears of a similar one during the one to come, it was urgently needed. A few months later Lyn Hewins undertook an organ-playing marathon in which she raised £133.

David Teagle reflected on financial matters in 1990. He thanked everyone for their help in raising funds for property repairs and for the new coffee lounge. The annual assessment had risen by over £3,000 to £10,164, a considerable amount for the Society to find. The following year, in 1991, David handed over the financial reins to Derek Skinner who held the post for 12 years, until 2003. But then, after a break of three years, Derek was back in post again.

The Caretaker

In 1907 complaints were received about door keeping, probably a role that was a part of the caretaker's duties. The Chapel Committee was urged to give the matter its immediate attention and to consider a proposal that four Stewards of Welcome should be appointed. It seems that the problem was not new as a meeting minute from many years before refers to one particular member of the congregation who was warned that if he persisted in entering the Chapel during prayers or the lesson then his pew would be taken from him.

In 1909 Mariah Skinner was the cleaner and Arthur Carveth was responsible for lighting the fires at one shilling per time. The caretaker's house was Number 50

Rosemundy Hill, in what is now the pedestrian access to the Chapel. Over the years John Lawrey, Arthur Estlick, and W T Curtis worked to keep it in good repair.

An interesting document dated December 1942 shows that the caretaker had a huge range of duties to perform in return for his or her rent-free accommodation and salary of £40 per year. The Revd Joe Ridholls recalled Russell and Lily Richards in the role. In 1970 it was taken over by Len Claydon who undertook the job until August 1986.

In 1986 the role was divided to separate the Chapel and the grounds. Mrs Joan Beckett took over the care of the former. When she retired in 1991 Mrs Hilary Wills became the cleaner, a position now held by Mrs Pat Ely.

Mrs Lily Richards receiving two cheques from the Revd Philip Williams to mark her retirement as caretaker at the Chapel. Also pictured are; *far left;* Albert Reynolds and *far right;* Redvers Bennetts.

The Wider Community

The Methodist Church in St Agnes has always sought to position itself at the heart of the community and as a reflection of this Mrs Semmens and Mrs Knox were appointed Chapel representatives to Rosemundy Home for unmarried mothers at the 1928 Annual Leaders Meeting, positions later held by the ministers.

In 1938 the Revd A G Payne and his young wife became the Chapel visitors to the Rosemundy Rescue Home. Their first child was born in St Agnes but they were only able to stay for about 18 months, as at the outbreak of war he became a military chaplain and was based in Malta when it was under continual threat from the Germans. Much later they returned and he became a supernumerary at Newlyn East.

Despite the involvement at Rosemundy the Revd Joe Ridholls felt that more could be done to make the mothers feel a part of the community during their stay in St Agnes. It was not simply rhetoric and during the late 1950s he and Joan invited small groups of them to come to tea at the Manse. Many attended and even now Joe can recall the poignancy of their stories.

The Chapel Poor Fund was available to provide some financial help for local families experiencing difficulties, before it was so readily available from the public purse. In 1941 there was a change in policy: instead of money, each of the 13 recipients received two bags of coal.

The talk of Sunday cinemas in St Agnes and Perranporth raised considerable concern amongst the members of the Methodist congregation in 1958. The cinemas were, of course, following the trend in the towns but out in the small villages there were fears that it would affect congregations and a petition was quickly organised.

The Luncheon Club began in 1999, a Methodist initiative which is still running. It is not restricted to church members but provides all senior citizens of the parish with the opportunity to enjoy an excellent monthly meal for a very modest cost. It is held in the Methodist hall, on two consecutive days, and the volunteer helpers greatly appreciate the new kitchen facilities.

On the Stage

A few members were keen on theatrical productions both for the youth groups and for senior members. The production of the play "The Vigil" on Good Friday in 1961 was one of these and was a spectacular success. It was based on the Easter miracle and as the programme said, "We open it every nightfall of Good Friday, in the courtroom of every modern man's mind."

Some members of the cast of 'The Vigil'.

Taking part were:

Elsie Vanstone - Mrs Harris
William Morrison - Night Watchman
Clyde Pope - The Judge
Noel Hoskins - The Prosecutor
Morley Nancarrow - Defence Counsel
Frank Kneebone - Clerk of the Court
Roy Blewett - Gardener and Defendant
Mary James - Esther a country girl
Keith Jeffery - Lucius a soldier
Thomas Tremewan - Joseph a wealthy lawyer
Margaret Roberts - Lady Procula the Governor's wife
Edwin Tredinnick - Pontius Pilate
David Bunney - Saul a Deputy
Maureen Sandercock - Beaulah a Barmaid
Roger Williams - Sadoc a Private Detective
June Lovering - Susannea a housewife
Lester Roberts - Thaddeus a professor
Margaret Davey - Magdalen a convert
Roger James - Peter a fisherman

"The Vigil" returned to the stage in the mid 1970s in a repeat of the play performed in the Chapel in 1961. This time the cast included:

Daphne Matthews	Roy Blewett
Len Clayton	Margaret Davey
Sydney Knight	Noel Hoskins
Peter Dodgson	Michael Hill
The Revd Ken Sadler	Ann Dodgson
Michael Curry	Edgar Penhaligon
Roger Williams	June Lovering
John Rive	Bill Cheshire
Judith Heyworth	Enid Jones
Frank Martin	Malcolm Carveth
Esther Cheshire	

Over the years there have been many drama productions by the members of St Agnes and wider Circuit Methodist Community. In April 1970 a group of local people was involved in an evening of dramatic readings from the works of Dorothy L Sayers: "Man born to be King."

Taking part were:

Betty Tredinnick	Margaret Davey	Richard Bamber
Noel Hoskins	Michael Fairhead	Robin Williams
David Pugsley	Marjorie Tonkin	Andrew Blewett
Roy Blewett	Elizabeth Pugsley	Kevin Benney
Roger Williams	Bernard Hoskins	Ann Beckett
Vivian Tonkin	Donald Campbell	Glynis Olds
Rex Easton	Brian Roberts	Malcolm Carveth
Peter Thomas	David Hawkes	Janet Carveth
Douglas Cockbein	Anthony Cheshire	David Teagle
George Heyworth	David Stevens	David Olds

The Coffee Lounge

In 1986 the Chapel was buzzing with Sunday school activities and Glynis Teagle expressed a wish to create a room where the teenagers could meet together in the evenings or after school, for a chat, and maybe do their homework. The dream grew. It was embraced by the whole church but instead of converting one of the old rooms the Trustees considered a much larger and more ambitious plan – a new coffee lounge.

It was to be an extension consisting of a modern kitchen and a beautifully furnished relaxation room, an informal meeting place for the young people and a much-needed facility for the wider community.

Most of the finance came from the Circuit and it was hoped that the new building would provide some ongoing rental income. Gordon Milner was responsible for the project and Bernard True of St Agnes was the builder. The final cost was about £40,000.

The Chapel c.1986 before the building of the new coffee lounge and showing the Preacher's vestry entrance.

It was a splendid addition to the facilities on offer but Margaret Hoskins and many others lamented the fact that the Planning Authority objected to the use of stonework with the result that its appearance is in stark contrast to the remainder of the Chapel.

Methodist Groups

Over the years a variety of groups have met under the umbrella of St Agnes Methodist Chapel. We have consulted a number of people to try and compile a comprehensive list, but it is probable that we have missed a few so we will offer our apologies now.

The Family Guild proved popular and on one occasion it began its season with a presentation by the "Praisemakers." Alex Nicholls referred to the involvement by the Senior Youth Group who hoped to form a judo group, hold a "Mini Olympics" and organise a Christmas Party.

"Network," formerly the Women's Fellowship and Women's Work, was a community of women of all ages who, through mission and service, sought to share Christ's love for the world. Margaret Hoskins recalled Granny Pope (Clyde's mother), Elsie Tredinnick and Miss MacDonald from Vicarage Road as hard-working members. In 1990 it was still attracting 18 regular members to each meeting and very much alive. A Knit-in for the Arthritic and Rheumatism Council was well supported and members contributed to the stalls at the Christmas Fayre. When it closed in December 1996, after 42 years, Muriel Kneebone had been its Secretary for the entire period.

With a theme of Fun, Friendship and Fellowship, the Ladies Monday Club started in 1978 and met on alternative Mondays. Dinah Teagle was its first President but gives credit to Kath Knight for the idea and for being its first Secretary; Glynis Teagle was the Treasurer. There was a speaker or visit arranged for each meeting and in February 1988 the group celebrated its 10th birthday with a special cake made by Jenny Osborne. The programme of speakers in the February 1987 newsletter included "The Work of the Macmillan Nursing Service" and "Java Nightmare." Two other topics guaranteed to excite the ladies were "Shopping through the Ages" and "Hats" (!!). In 1998 the group celebrated its 20th birthday but at Christmas 2001 it closed.

The Revd Steven Emery and Jenny Osborne began the "Think and Drink" discussion group in 1988 when members met over a cup of tea on Tuesday mornings. Jenny also formed "New Dimension," a social group of about 20 members who met for walks and get-togethers including a themed party of "Sinking of the Titanic." Unfortunately this group only lasted for about three years but "Think and Drink" still meets weekly.

Liz Thorley started the Craft Group. About a dozen people from the Chapel meet once a month to expand their creative talents by painting on glass and silk, making cards and jewellery and trying their hands at a whole host of other activities. The first show of the St Agnes Methodist Art Group was held in August 1997. It proved to be a great success and various items were sold to provide funds for the Chapel refurbishment.

The "Christian Care Group" began in December 1988, firstly within the Methodist Chapel but then widened into an ecumenical group. Within a couple of years it had raised over £1,500 through coffee mornings and a range of other events. Many causes have benefited from its efforts including Water Aid, Shelterbox and the Asian Tsunami appeal. It still holds three coffee mornings a year for different charities and aims to respond to emergencies, as when in early 2009 it raised £650 for the children of Gaza and in January 2010, £1,050 for Haiti. For many years it has provided a Christmas party for the Gateway Club of Truro for over 100 people. It also provided and served lunch once a month in the MacMillan Centre in Truro until it closed.

"WOW" began in 2006. No, it wasn't a pop group, it stood for Worship on Wednesday and the Revd Joan Watson explained that it offered a contemporary mix of praise and worship, Bible study and prayer. It was for all ages and met on one evening per week. It was the forerunner of her present Bible Study which currently meets on Wednesday afternoons and Thursday mornings. In addition, there are three other Bible Study Groups meeting on Mondays, Tuesdays and Wednesdays.

In addition the Methodist premises are used regularly by the Floral Art Club, Gardening Club, the Old Cornwall Society, Healing Place, Not so Young Club, Weight Watchers, St Julia's Hospice Group amongst others. There are also many organisations that use it occasionally. From this it can be appreciated that the Chapel is used extensively for secular purposes as well as for worship. It is home to many voluntary organisations and caters for all ages including the Chapel Youth Department, so important for the future. The Methodist Society is proud of its open-door policy and of its warm and friendly welcome to all who cross its threshold whether it is for a community gathering or to take part in a religious service.

We finish this chapter with a simple question of what the Chapel means to the community. In response Brian Roberts thought about the various aspects of Chapel life: the sermons, the visiting great and good, the special events, the building and its changes. But for him the people were more important than all of this. He said, "Perhaps not all were especially religious but they made you feel welcome whatever your background or appearance. I think of these people as always smiling but I'm not sure they always were, several had real hardships and indeed tragedies to cope with. What I do know is that the village was a better place because of them; they had a way of making a person feel they belonged. Maybe, in their small way, they were building the Kingdom of God here in our midst."

l-r; Dinah Teagle, June Lovering, Revd Steven Emery, Denise Rogers, Esther Cheshire outside the newly built Coffee Lounge.

Band of Hope

Jabez Tunnicliff formed the Band of Hope in Leeds, in 1847. Its main purpose was to combat the evil of alcohol and through its work it sought to teach children the importance and principles of sobriety and teetotalism. In 1855 it went national with meetings in churches throughout the country.

For the leaders of this group the early fight was against the influence of public houses and brewers as it set out to rescue those whose lives had been affected by drink. At a time when so many families were blighted by the effects of alcohol, Methodists welcomed it as a positive step in teaching total abstinence and it came to be seen as closely related to the Methodist Church. Elsewhere in the country alcohol-free premises were established and rallies,

The Band of Hope tea at Goonown in 1907.

The Band of Hope tea in 1908.

marches and demonstrations were held to oppose the evils of hard liquor. As an alternative, coffee taverns were set up to keep teetotallers true to their pledge.

'Signing the pledge' was its main feature. Members were asked to make the promise, "I do agree that I will not use intoxicating liquor as beverages." Clive Benney, in his book "Around St Agnes," said, "Some societies even mentioned tobacco, snuff and opium. Many started within existing Sunday schools but most children lapsed their pledge on reaching maturity." Millions of people made the promise to abstain from alcohol, encouraged by lectures, magic lantern shows and by noted personalities invited to speak at public meetings in support of the cause.

By 1935 the movement had nearly 3,000,000 members but by the early 1950s society had changed and its appeal had diminished.

The Band of Hope was active in St Agnes for many years and at its 1906 annual demonstration evening the

The Band of Hope tea treat procession at Churchtown in 1912.

Revd G W Thompson and Mrs Billing gave the address. Senior members provided recitations and Miss Williams conducted the juvenile choir.

Like the Wesleyans they also held their tea treats. The members paraded through the village and usually ended up in a field adjoining Goonown Farm, owned by the Butson family. In May 1907 the "Royal Cornwall Gazette" reported that the annual demonstration of the Goonown Band of Hope took place on Whit Monday and was headed by Trevince Band. Councillor Fellowes of Wolverhampton led the evening meeting and the Revds G W Thompson, W G Corke and Mr M J Angwin gave the addresses.

We have not found any reference to the body being discontinued but the September 1909 meeting of the St Agnes Wesleyan Society referred to a resolution that the Band of Hope be recommended and in May of the following year St Agnes Silver Band led the parade for the

Goonown Band of Hope annual tea. The members paraded the streets before returning to a field at Goonown. John Angwin conducted the choir of 20 voices in the evening concert.

In June 1914 the annual festival was held in what was described as favourable conditions. The "West Briton" newspaper reported that the children met in Goonown schoolroom and after a hymn and prayer they formed a procession and, headed by St Agnes Band, they paraded the principal streets. The procession passed through the beautiful grounds of Rosemundy and then returned to Mr A Butson's field at Goonown where the children had their buns and tea.

In 1915 the First World War was in progress. A number of local men were away fighting for their country and the Chapel leaders asked the Band of Hope to arrange a concert on behalf of the Christmas Pudding Fund for the soldiers serving at the front. A reference to the St Agnes Band of Hope was found for the year 1925 but, sadly, we have no further information on it.

The Band of Hope tea in 1913.

Sunday School (Youth Department)

Robert Raikes (1736 – 1811), an Anglican, is credited with starting the Sunday school movement in Britain, in 1780; it was a school for boys from the slums. Sunday was the obvious choice as the boys were working the other six days. They were taught reading, writing, numeracy and religion; the teachers were lay people and their textbooks included the Bible. Gradually more schools opened and the movement was extended to include girls.

The schools were derisively called "Raikes' Ragged Schools." They had their critics including those who complained that they weakened religious education in the home but by 1831 Sunday schools in Great Britain were teaching over a million children each week.

The first 100 years or so

The Methodist Sunday school in St Agnes was opened in 1809, at Goonown Chapel, but according to Bill Morrison, the Anglican Sunday school here pre-dates it by 23 years. He recorded that in 1786 the St Agnes curate, the Revd William Harpur, wrote to the "Sherbourne Mercury" newspaper claiming that his Sunday school, supported by the local mines, was the first in Cornwall.

According to the 1964 Chapel re-opening programme, the teachers met in February 1834 to appoint a Superintendent: Mr James Waters. He took the place of Mr Joseph Waters who had been asked to relinquish the office because of his rare attendance to the duties. The programme also recorded that in July of that year there were 111 boys and 84 girls being taught by 16 male and 18 female teachers. The school was thriving and to accommodate the numbers Goonown Chapel was enlarged twice during the 19th century. By 1888 the numbers had increased further and there were 154 boys and 161 girls attending the Sunday gatherings.

In his Journal, local boy John Carter (1835-1907) wrote, "I was taken to the Goonown Sunday school when about five years old. The leading men there in my early days were George Rogers, Thomas Whitta, Capt. Joseph Ninnis, Thomas Ninnis, James Stephens and others. In that school many characters were made, scores of young men were moulded and fashioned for responsible positions in various parts of the world and so they have gone out to almost every part of the habitable globe doing credit to their homes and all their early surroundings. We had no organ but generally there would be one or more flutes, sometimes a clarinet, one or two bass-violins, a trombone and serpent but I never knew a violin in church worship in Cornwall. All this time I was a very regular attendant at the Goonown Sunday school and for a good while was in the Bible Class; my near associates were William Endean of Truro, William Webb and John Hosking of Polbreen. Captain Joseph Ninnis and Thomas Ninnis were my teachers. George Rogers was the Superintendent, our school numbered over three hundred scholars and about fifty teachers."

By 1859 the Sunday school had been running for 50 years and a set of medals was struck to celebrate its golden jubilee.

Revd Joe Ridholls watches as members of the Boys' Brigade tuck into their meal.

The Boys' Brigade

In 1906 the Chapel leaders let it be known that if the Sunday school officers and teachers wished to establish a Boys' Brigade then no objection would be raised. We are not certain that the idea came to fruition but many years later, sometime around 1960, the Revd Joe Ridholls certainly did start a unit. He was its Captain and Chaplain and young Malcolm Carveth was one of his recruits.

The Classes of the 1920s and 1930s

In 1920, local Policeman Richard Henry Benney, Clive Benney's great-grandfather, left St Agnes bound for Illogan Highway where he became involved with the Chapel. He had been active in the Chapel and Sunday school at St Agnes for many years, as general Superintendent of the senior school and as the Treasurer of the tea treat fund. In appreciation of his services at St Agnes he was presented with an inscribed Bible.

From the Class Books we can tell that there were 131 members of the Sunday school in June 1923. There were also a further five junior members and one on trial.

Richie Sandercock of Goonown joined the mixed primary class in 1928, at the age of four. He moved to Lester Robert's junior boys' class three years later and at twelve years of age he joined the seniors. He said, "Doris Ward, Ada Oats and Elsie Vanstone prepared the children for the concerts and I particularly liked the comb band. The pitch depended on the spacing of the comb teeth." No doubt good training for his time in St Agnes Silver Band.

St Agnes girl, Margaret Davey, attended Sunday school at Goonown from 1930 and recalled the boys and girls being taught in separate classes. She said, "The primary class was in a side room with the junior to adult classes in

Young Richie Sandercock eats a Tea Treat saffron bun in the late 1920s.

Frank Roberts of Goonown attended from 1926 to 1939. He recalled Father Christmas, complete with presents, descending from the hatch in the ceiling. For years he wondered how he had managed to climb up without being seen and then one day he discovered a second hatch above the balcony and the mystery was solved.

the main hall. Mrs Pengelly, the stationmaster's wife, held a class for a large number of young men. The building was very cold with the only heating from a tortoise stove; you had to wrap up well. Will Butson and Luther Stephens were the Secretaries, they ticked our names each week. An attendance mark was important as your prize at the end of the year depended on it."

The Annual Teachers' Meeting minutes of 1935 held in Goonown Schoolroom show that there was a considerable team leading the youngsters. Apart from the many teachers there were four senior school pianists and Mr L Stephens, the Temperance Secretary.

One day some news arrived which shocked the entire Sunday school: young Edith Grigg from Goonown had been killed when her brakes failed as she rode her bicycle down St George's Hill, Perranporth. She was a senior member of the Sunday school and a popular girl.

The Move to a New Home
In 1939 the Army requisitioned Goonown Schoolroom for the war effort. The Sunday school collected together its equipment and transferred to St Agnes Chapel in British Road. Margaret Davey was one of the teachers and recalled that the new arrangement was far from ideal. "The sessions were held on Sunday afternoons with classes in the back vestry and in the Chapel. The pews were uncomfortable and conditions cramped. With so many groups sharing the available space it required a lot of tolerance and co-operation. There were four classes: the beginners, primary, juniors and teenagers. Lester and Margaret Roberts, Reg Roberts (the Postmaster) and Clyde Pope were among the teachers."

At the AGM in 1945 it was agreed to "use the Chapel for our Sunday school meetings a little longer until something definite is known regarding Goonown." There were those who held out the hope that the Sunday school could return to its former home but two years later it was concluded that as the old hall was not a suitable place in its present state, classes would remain at St Agnes.

The Classes of the 1940s and 1950s

In September 1942 Mr Jim Solomon offered to organise a Young People's Fellowship. It was eagerly accepted and he was promised all the facilities needed.

Noel Hoskins from Silverwell became involved as a teacher in the early 1940s and six years later he became Superintendent. Noel made a major contribution to the Sunday school and took a lead in the introduction of the Methodist Concise Guide, a structured approach to tuition. In 1946 Noel's wife, Margaret, joined him as a teacher. She later became group leader for the primary and beginners; Thelma Bunt, Eileen Hoare (Harold Hoare's sister) and Doreen Clissold also taught this age group. Another of the teachers from the 1940s was Roy Blewett; in 1946 he was teaching the scholars aged 14 and over in number one vestry.

The annual meeting of 1946 was referred to in the minute book as the Annual Meeting of Officers and Teachers of St Agnes Methodist Sunday School. By the following year it had become the Annual Meeting of the Youth Council and in subsequent years as the Sunday School Council. Either by design or by accident the name seemed to be changing but it had little effect, the term Sunday school remained in use for many years after.

Colin Butson became a member at the age of four, in 1947. He attended Goonbell in the morning and St Agnes in the afternoon where his teachers were Thelma Bunt and Mrs Phyllis Pharaoh. A few years later he joined the class of Harold Hoare, a young man who had made a good impression on Colin and the other youngsters in the age group nine to eleven – no doubt because he was a good footballer in the St Agnes team and was seen as a local celebrity. Harold's mother was Ivy Hoare, Jack Boundy's sister.

Sunday school class of 1947.

Susan Pope (Clyde Pope's daughter) and Maureen Sandercock taught the primary group and Mrs Mollard provided the piano accompaniment for about four years until replaced by Mrs Butcher. Margaret Hoskins recalled Clyde Pope giving her the ultimate accolade when her young class sang during one of the services: he turned to her and said, "Spot on." She also remembered her daughter, Janet, becoming impatient to leave for home. Margaret told her to have a little patience, to which Clyde remarked, "And where is she going to get that from, I wonder?" Margaret conceded that neither Noel nor she was blessed with a lot of patience.

Bill Morrison became the Sunday school Superintendent in 1951. The role entailed a fairly steep learning curve for him and every Tuesday evening he and the other teachers met for study. Bill wrote, "Reg Roberts had been a mainstay for thirty years and had served in the same role. Reg, his brother Lester, Clyde Pope, Ada Oates, Elsie Vanstone: all these and the Bible study for the next lesson taught me so much." Bill had a strong band of leaders including his wife, Christine, John Berryman's daughter. By 1957 Bill had been the Superintendent for six years. There were pressures on his life outside of St Agnes Chapel and he reluctantly announced that he would have to stand down but perhaps it would be for just a while. Reg Roberts stepped in to take up the reins again. After a break of only one year Bill Morrison was back as Superintendent. It was during this time that he played a part in the formation of the Sunday school at Cameron Estate.

The Sunday school was now flourishing with almost 120 members at its Sunday afternoon meetings. There were about 20 beginners squeezed into one small room, 40 primary members in the vestry at the back, 15 older

Nativity play c.1955 'Sunrise over Bethlehem'. *l-r;* David Boundy, Charlie Tamlyn, Harold Hoare, Kathleen Boundy, David Payne, Margaret Thomas, Ernest Thomas, Christopher Williams, Roger Williams, John Weezleman, ?, Elsie Vanstone, Kay Thewlis, ?, June Kneebone. *Front row, l-r;* Susan Kneebone, Marilyn Weeway, Elizabeth Williams, Roger James, Margaret Payne.

Sunday school in the late 1950s. *Back row, l-r;* Peter Roberts, Christopher Fabray, Peter Thomas; *Front row, l-r;* Paul Renfree, Neil Roberts, Ewart Butson, Kingsley Thomas, Rex Berryman.

The Revd Ambrose Payne Methodist Minister at St Agnes 1953 - 1957.

youngsters in the upstairs vestry and the remainder scattered around the pews of the Chapel. The Revd Ambrose Payne observed that the Sunday school was operating under difficult and cramped conditions; he stressed the urgent need for more adequate accommodation.

In 1959 St Agnes Methodist Sunday school celebrated its 150th anniversary. The Revd Wilfred Wade, Chairman of the Cornwall Methodist District, conducted the anniversary service on the 14th June and the programme stated that at least six generations had passed through the school with many of the former members among the countless "Cousin Jacks" around the world. It also posed the question of how many had become preachers, class-leaders or Sunday school teachers.

Sometime around 1959 the St Agnes Methodist minister, the Revd Joe Ridholls, with the help of Daphne Dunstan, formed a youth club at Goonown Schoolroom. It was referred to as the St Agnes Wesley Youth Centre and about 60 youngsters attended the weekly meetings. Joe said, "Roy Worgan, the county official, visited us on one occasion: it was not long after we had formed." It seems that Mr Worgan was very complimentary about the club including the physical training provided. A large variety of activities was on offer including toy-making, dancing, games and music in the form of a skiffle group.

The Revd Joe Ridholls recalled the arrival of a new piece of apparatus – a vaulting horse. "I decided that I could not expect the youngsters to use it unless I had tried it myself. I didn't want an audience so I went to the hall late at night. I set it up, prepared myself and began my run up. As I leapt onto the springboard I knew exactly where I had to place my hands but it didn't quite work out as planned. I slipped and tumbled to the floor. I lay there panting, unable to move for a full ten minutes. As I limped home I wondered who would have found me if I had broken my leg."

The Revd Joe Ridholls said, "Roy Worgan had travelled to Goonown by train and after the meeting I accompanied him back to the railway halt. As the train approached we waved to the driver. He must have been a particularly friendly chap because he waved back – and carried straight on. I had to take Mr Worgan back to Truro by car."

The Tea Treat procession along Vicarage Road in 1908 with the banner proudly carried at the front.

Tea Treats and Outings

John Kinsman, in his publication "The Cornish Handbook" referred to Whitsuntide festivals in Cornwall when "maidens and youths displayed their new clothes." He said, "Many villages held their 'Tea Drinking' on Whit-Monday. It was the time for lovers to walk together and to indicate their preferences to their neighbours. A 'Tea Drinking' is essentially a social function, enabling all who take part to dispense with the formalities which would normally keep them apart. First of all, a procession is formed, headed by a brass band and resplendent with banners and flags. After parading the village it enters a field, lent for the occasion by a friendly farmer. Men, women and children sit down to eat huge quantities of saffron cake (saffron buns) and drink freshly-made tea, the adults at long tables and the children on seats arranged to form a complete circle. Each child brings his or her own 'Tea Drinking' cup, which is emblazoned with some suitable motto; the tea is poured from huge earthenware pitchers, while saffron cakes are served from wide wicker baskets, each child receiving a whole cake. After tea, music and games fill the hours. The custom is so full of gladness that one hopes it may never be forgotten."

Tea treats have been largely confined to history and it may be that younger readers will not appreciate their significance to the church, chapel and community. Everything stopped for the occasion; it was the biggest event on the calendar. The venue was usually someone's large garden or a suitable field. The grass was cut, decorations erected and tables placed in position as stalls or for the food. In the early years brass bands stood to play but later, the schoolroom forms were dragged out and placed in concert formation.

As John Kinsman said, the event started with a procession. The Chapel banner was proudly carried at the front as a demonstration of the members' faith and identity. Immediately behind was the band, followed by the children and then the adults. Eventually the procession returned to the tea treat field and the band took its place on the wooden forms in readiness for the official opening. A local dignitary usually opened the day and the band began its afternoon programme. For much of the time there were very few listening but the occasional burst of applause made it all seem worthwhile. To this background music the children played games and sports. There were all sorts of goodies for them to buy: fruit, sweets (nicies as they were once called) little toys and ice cream, a rare delight in the early days before refrigeration was generally in use.

At some convenient point the children were given their tea treat bun, surely larger than the ones in the shops today, and whatever else people remembered about the day it was those buns.

Both the St Agnes Wesleyan Sunday school and the Band of Hope held annual tea treats; in the case of the latter it was often referred to as a "demonstration." The two events were organised by their respective leaders but

Tea was a high spot and when the children had finished it was the turn of the bandsmen, and no matter how hungry (or greedy) they were, the food just kept on coming. There were savouries, splits and cream and all sorts of fancy cakes, most of them homemade. No committee worth its salt was going to send a band home hungry and the acceptance of the engagement the following year was often based on the players' memory of the tea.

top; Tea Treat procession at Peterville in 1904.

above; Fairground rides at the 1904 Tea Treat celebrations.

many children attended both. The Wesleyan event was usually held in a field in Penwinnick Road, where Penwinnick Parc is today, but for a few years, towards the end of the First World War and probably just after, it was held in the small field opposite Coulterville (Cleaderscroft) in British Road, kindly loaned by Mr Coulter Hancock.

Despite our memories of the weather the sun did not always shine and on Saturday the 19th July 1902 the tea treat was postponed because of stormy and wet weather. But the children did not miss out: it was re-arranged for the following Monday afternoon when they were released early from school. According to the "Royal Cornwall Gazette" the Wesleyan tea in July 1904 was one of the most successful for many years. The weather was good and a large number of scholars and teachers paraded the streets with Camborne Town Band at the head.

The year 1909 was special as it was the Sunday school centenary, (the school had started in 1809) and the "Royal Cornwall Gazette" reported that the tea treat had attracted a large number of old scholars who had joined the procession. The children under eighteen years of age were given a free tea and officers, teachers and scholars were presented with a medal especially struck for the occasion. Truro Territorial Band and St Agnes Silver Band were on hand to provide the musical entertainment.

In July 1910 the "Royal Cornwall Gazette" reported that the weather had unfortunately interfered with the success of the Wesleyan Sunday school tea. However, it did not prevent it from being held and St Agnes Silver and the illustrious St Dennis were the preferred bands. The following year the Illogan Reed and Brass Band was in attendance under the baton of the Revd H Oxland. As well as taking part in sports and games, the children were able to join in maypole dancing, singing and recitation competitions. Mr Oxland and the Illogan Reed and Brass Band were back again in 1912 so they must have made a good sound the previous year.

The Sunday school centenary in 1909 was marked with the issue of another medal.

top; Tea Treat procession at Churchtown in 1909.

above; Tea Treat procession at Churchtown in 1910.

The 1913 procession was described as a "garland" occasion. The "Royal Cornwall Gazette" reported that the endless variety of shapes and sizes of garlands of beautiful flowers made a very pretty sight. It was again held in Mr Peters' field at Penwinnick where former scholars both from home and South Africa provided the tea. There was a good entry in the sports and St Dennis Band was back to provide the music.

Children eat their large saffron buns at the 1913 Tea Treat.

The event in 1914 was held against the background of a country heading for war. It was also partly spoilt by rain but, as ever, it provided the opportunity for a re-union of old friends. Illogan Reed and Brass Band led the procession which was described as "below average because counter attractions drew children away from sports and games." The report does not say what the counter attractions were.

On the 20th August 1919 the "Royal Cornwall Gazette" reported: "The annual gathering on Friday of the Sunday school was a great success. There was the usual procession, headed by St Agnes Band under Mr H Robins,

White table cloths on trestle tables for the Sunday School tea in 1914.

around the grounds of Rosemundy and the principal streets to the field lent by Mr G C Hancock where tea was served. A free tea was provided for the children and the ex-servicemen whilst the older members of the Chapel and the sick were not forgotten. In the sports that followed the young people thoroughly enjoyed themselves." Another report stated that Redruth Band was in attendance so despite it being a time of austerity, it would seem that funds were sufficient for two bands.

The biggest outlay for tea treats was for the brass band. It was an essential element of the day as it led the procession and provided the entertainment. The extent of the cost depended on whether one of the major bands like St Dennis or Camborne had been booked. The fee was usually covered by a collection in advance of the event when Chapel members, mostly ladies according to Margaret Davey, went out with their little receipt books and collected contributions ranging from a few pence to

ST AGNES WESLEYAN S. SCHOOL TEA. July 11 1920.   No. 2.

Tea Treat procession along Vicarage Road outside the Men's Institute in 1920.

two shillings and sixpence (12.5p). Margaret said, "The tea treat was the big occasion of the summer; in my day it was the third Saturday in July. The band was booked, it could have been Redruth or Lanner or even St Dennis if we could afford them. We would all wear our best clothes, maybe a new dress. I remember the races and, of course, the saffron buns the size of a tea plate. There is nothing to compare with it these days, and they were washed down with a cup of sweet tea. An elderly gentleman arrived at noon to make a fire in a sheltered corner of the field. He placed a large urn on it and filled it with water collected from neighbouring houses. He kept this boiling all day. The men brought large earthenware pitchers from which they served the tea. The tables were beautifully laid with ornate teapots, hot water jugs and other crockery. There were splits, sponges, cakes; everything was homemade. The day ended with the Serpentine Walk. I've been told that many romances began with this as the young men chose their dancing partner. They walked in a circle which became tighter and tighter until the leader reversed and led everyone out of the maze."

In 1947 there was a seaside outing rather than a tea treat but that decision did not signal the end of the traditional gathering that we now look back on with so much nostalgia. In 1953 it was the old-fashioned tea treat again, in the field off Penwinnick Road. The decision was to book Camborne Town Band if it was available: failing that it was to be either Newquay or Stithians. The minutes record that all the jobs were allocated including the important task of purchasing the 6oz saffron buns (that's strange, they were 8oz in 1917!)

In 1959 the sound of the traditional brass band gave way to the Band of the 1st Camborne Company of the Boys' Brigade. Probably best not to comment any further about the sound except to say that the lads did a good job of leading the procession to the usual field at Penwinnick Road.

Throughout the 1960s, 1970s and 1980s the members enjoyed an annual trip to the beach. Two, sometimes three, coaches were hired to take them and their parents to destinations around Cornwall: Padstow, Marazion, Falmouth, Carbis Bay and St Ives were the most popular. In the early years the local chapel hall was hired where a splendid tea was provided. In later years hot pasties were delivered in time for lunch with regular cries of, "When are the pasties coming?" Eventually the smell of freshly baked pasties heralded the arrival of the traditional Cornish feast.

Picnic teas ended the day. The children arrived home, tired, perhaps a little sunburnt, but with happy memories of a day spent with family and friends. Even today folk can be heard reminiscing about the Sunday school outings.

The tea treat of 1978 was an important milestone as it was the first joint event involving both the Methodists and Anglicans. Fittingly, it was our local St Agnes Silver Band that led the long procession to Beaconsfield.

Bill Cheshire and Donald Tremain led the 1984 tea treat

Beach games and sandcastle building competitions occupied the afternoon and it was not unknown for some of the more competitive dads to smuggle garden spades and other building equipment onto the beach in an effort to win the prize.

procession with Gary Springall carrying the banner. At 3.00 o'clock St Agnes Silver Band struck up a march and the parade moved off on its way to Enys' Park Football Field for the sports and competitions. St Agnes Old Cornwall Society rounded off the day with a bonfire on the Beacon.

As a part of the 250th anniversary of Wesley's conversion June Lovering included an item in the April 1988 newsletter about the celebration tea treat. It involved the Methodist Churches of St Agnes, Mount Hawke and Trevellas, the Parish Churches of St Agnes and Mount Hawke and the St Agnes Roman Catholic Church. It turned out to be a splendid event with a procession and family day at Goonown Playing Fields with stalls, side shows, Punch and Judy, family tea and, of course, the traditional tea treat buns and Serpentine Walk.

It seems that you cannot kill off a good idea and it is good to see tea treats being revived. It was not the first ecumenical version in St Agnes but the 2008 event at

The ecumenical Tea Treat procession at Peterville in 1988.

Goonown Playing Field was a great success. It was repeated in 2009. Joan Watson said that the weather was amazing and that everyone had a wonderful time with food in abundance, all provided by the parents and helpers from the Church and Chapel. The smiling faces in the scores of photographs provide the proof that everyone enjoyed it.

Drama and Music
Frank Roberts did not enjoy being on stage but during the late 1920s, when he was six or seven years old, he was talked into it. His Aunt Eda, Reg Trezise's wife, the organist, paired him up with her daughter, Josephine, to sing the duet "Where are you going, my pretty maid?" All went well until the day of the performance. The people were in their seats – waiting. Frank and Josephine were back-stage, it was tense, they were about to make their grand debut. Frank said, "I suddenly thought how silly I looked and no amount of coaxing would get me onto the stage.

'Goody 2 Shoes' performed in 1975.

'Little Red Riding Hood'.

Josephine had to go ahead with Betty Fletcher taking my part." Poor Frank's theatrical career was at an end.

Noel Hoskins, Roy Blewett, Will Sheaff, Edna Rundell and Mabel Trezise formed a Youth Guild in the 1950s and Margaret Hoskins said, "Out of this came a strong drama group. Mrs Shrimpton was its first director, she had previously worked on the London Stage and brought with her considerable dramatic experience. Noel was very keen and involved himself in most of the productions. They were performed each year at St Agnes Chapel and then taken around the other chapels in the Circuit."

Kathleen Miles returned to St Agnes in the early 1970s and brought with her an experience of song and dance. Also returning home, to Promised Land from Redruth, were Bill and Esther Cheshire. Bill, in particular, was well known for his Scouting Gang Shows and for his involvement with Redruth Amateur Operatic Society Trust. All three became actively involved in the Sunday school. In 1974 the Church welcomed a new minister, the Revd Ken Sadler and his wife, Joyce. She helped with the stage productions and, together with the existing talent, made a very strong and able team. Very soon the "Methodist Players" was formed.

The nativity play in 1992 brought a surprise for one family: Richard and Sue Houghton had settled down to enjoy the performance but within minutes they were on their way to the casualty department at Treliske Hospital. Their 10 year-old son, David, was to have played the part of the innkeeper but just before the curtain rose he had tripped over a shepherd's crook and broken his wrist. Multi-talented Glynis Teagle stepped in to take over the role.

Bill Cheshire loved Pantomime and at St Agnes in 1985 he led the production of "Cinderella." He announced that he was delighted with the rehearsals and that the show would run for three nights. Unfortunately the weather had other ideas. The following year it was "Aladdin" and after the snow-affected production of 1985 the cast kept their fingers crossed. "Dick Whittington" was chosen for 1987 and the huge cast of seventy must have presented some problems during rehearsals. "Jack and the Beanstalk" followed in 1988 and the following year it was "Sleeping Beauty."

The year 1988 was celebrated in considerable style with a production of "Joseph and the Amazing Technicolor Dreamcoat." It was a superb performance with Emma Reed as the singing narrator and Mark Davidson playing the part of Joseph. Singing too was popular; a youth choir was formed and membership quickly grew to 60; a successful year culminated in a performance at the famous Gwennap Pit in front of 500 people.

'Joseph and the Amazing Technicolour Dreamcoat' in 1994.

The West End returned to St Agnes in 1994 with a repeat production of the musical "Joseph and the Amazing Technicolor Dreamcoat," produced by Glynis Teagle and Christine Roberts. It played to packed audiences for three nights and was repeated during carnival week in August. The large cast comprised members of the Methodist Youth Sections and St Agnes Parish Church. Alison Williams was choreographer and Pam Williams provided the costume expertise. Jeffrey Knight played the part of Joseph and Anna Butterfield was the narrator. James Fogg, James McCaslin, James Euden, Daniel Rosenfeld, Matthew Howley, Guy Renfree, Jonathan Howley, Daniel Prisk, Robin Teagle, Ian Bucknole and Paul Solomon were Joseph's brothers. Suzannah Teagle, David Barker, Martin Richards, Andrew Dunn, Debbie Austin, David Olds, Robin Mason and David Crocker provided the musical accompaniment.

'God's Big Top'.

There Was Sport Too
Turning to sport we read that it was Falmouth against St Agnes in April 1948 when the Youth Guild responded to a challenge on the hockey pitch. The records show that

St Agnes was victorious but there is nothing written about the return match in May. Perhaps it was best forgotten.

During the late 1980s the members took part in various District sporting events. The junior football team, coached by David Teagle, proved a force to be reckoned with. The senior netball teams, coached by Jan Roberts, and the senior 5 a-side football teams, again coached by David, had successes in winning district competitions and went on to represent Cornwall in the regional MAYC competitions. In June 1990 the Netball team travelled to Bristol to compete in the regional finals, just one occasion when the hard-working leaders took the youngsters across the Tamar.

On the 10th June 1988 a group of young people took part in a sponsored keep-fit in aid of Muscular Dystrophy. They skipped, hula hooped, leap-frogged, somersaulted and danced from 7.00pm to 7.00am to raise £500. Claire Thorley organised the event which involved Emma Laity, Sarah Millbank, Lisa Murrish, Rachel Osborne, Emma Roberts, Tamsin Thomas, Alison White, Claire Thorley, Justin Nicholls, Kittow Hocking, Alex Cockle, Frank Gane, Richard Atkinson and not forgetting, of course, gymnast extraordinaire, the Revd Steven Emery.

The Classes of the 1960s and 1970s

In October 1960 a visit by the Revd Reg Bedford from the Methodist Youth Department and Jon West, the County Youth Organiser, brought many young people to the parish for a weekend conference entitled "On the Spot." The Revd Joe Ridholls, the St Agnes Minister and Cornwall Methodist Youth Club District Secretary, arranged a full programme of events which began at the Porthvean Hotel. From there the delegates set out to visit many of the clubs in the area and ended up at Silverwell for a splendid tea. The Sunday included services and discussions and the event was brought to a close with a youth rally in St Agnes Chapel attended by about 600 people from many local organisations including the Boys' Brigade and Threemilestone Young Farmers' Club led by its Chairman, Roger Williams, a prominent Chapel and youth worker at St Agnes. Also represented were Perranporth, Porthtowan and St Agnes Surf Life Saving Clubs. Mr C H J Hicks, who invented the Hicks Life-Saving Reel, was also there. St Agnes Silver Band provided some of the musical accompaniment and Miss Wendy Lewis, the John o' Groats to Land's End walker, gave a talk on the value of living a Christian life. She also presented proficiency certificates to members of the St Agnes SLSC.

Sometime around 1960 the idea of a Central Methodist Secondary Sunday school was floated. It was to be held at the new Chapel at Trevellas and Crosscoombe with members taken there by coach, free of charge. Letters outlining the scheme and signed by G A Parrott (Superintendent), J A D Ridholls (Youth Secretary) and W H Morrison were sent to parents. Betty Tredinnick recalled the meeting to discuss the proposals. She said that there was a large attendance, mostly to record a firm "No." Perhaps, understandably, few wanted to see the demise of their own Sunday schools but that was exactly what happened as within a few years most in the Circuit had closed.

In the early 1960s a shortage of teachers was causing concern. The drive to find more helpers did not meet with much success so to overcome the immediate problem there was a shuffling of roles and a number of the senior girls were encouraged to become helpers.

When work began on the major Chapel alterations in 1964, for about six months, the classes met in a number of private homes. It might not have been the best way to run a large Sunday school but there was the promise of much better facilities to come. The alterations opened a new chapter in the life of the Sunday school. Everyone could now meet together under the same roof, at the same time and with adequate space. The youngsters were able to join in the first part of the morning worship and

The new Friday Night Youth Club c. 1965. *back l-r;* Christopher Morrison, Paul Renfree, Ewart Butson, *middle row;* Andrew Langham, Barry Spring, Kingsley Thomas, Malcolm Carveth, David Prime, *front row;* Pat Smith (leader), Dianne Langham, Liz Williams, Janet Hoskins, Anne Claydon, Lesley Hoskins.

then go "downstairs" to their classes. The beginners, primary, juniors and seniors had their own rooms.

The new hall also made it possible to hold a youth club which met on Friday nights. If offered the usual range of club activities including table tennis, darts, and five-a-side football. Leaders Pat and Bill Smith also produced sketch shows and reviews, making full use of the new stage.

During the late 1960s a Sunday Night Youth Fellowship group was formed which met at Bill and Christine Morrison's house. Bill, a former Sunday school Superintendent and teacher, had become a local preacher. Young people from this group accompanied him to his services, taking an active role in the readings, sermons and singing. The young people were indebted to the love, care and example shown by the Morrison family who opened up their home every Sunday night and

The Sunday night Youth Fellowship group c.1967. *back l-r;* Felicia Johns, Lesley Hoskins, Glynis Olds, *front row; l-r* Janet Olds, Susan Kneebone, David Teagle, Peter Thomas.

supplied them with endless chocolate biscuits and other refreshments. The group continued for many years, providing the Church with a strong youth section, a plentiful supply of Sunday school teachers and two marriages – Janet and Malcolm Carveth and Glynis and David Teagle.

Tragedy rocked the group in April 1972 from which it never fully recovered. In his book, "Jack of all Trades," Bill Morrison talks of the Circuit-sponsored walk in which his 14 year-old son, Martin, was killed. The walk was in aid of Overseas Missions and the young people of St Agnes Chapel had been keen to do their bit. A young driver lost control of his car and ploughed into Martin. It was a shock that extended far beyond the Methodist community. The Chapel was packed for the funeral and the village came to a standstill. The Revd Philip Williams described the period as, "…clearly amongst the most challenging in the whole of my ministry."

Following this accident, together with the fact that several members were now married and others had left for university, the group ceased to meet but the strong links forged within it are still in place to this day and the young people will always be grateful for the example and witness of Bill and Christine Morrison.

David Rees became the Superintendent in 1975; he described his six years in the role as the most fulfilling of his life. He said, "Each Sunday about 15 to 20 of the senior members gathered at our house for an informal meeting. On our return from evening service we would find them waiting on our doorstep. They had their tea and biscuits and stayed for an hour or so. During the summer months it was more likely to be a barbecue or bonfire."

In 1977 it was decided to hold a competition for a new Sunday school banner. It had to have the name of the Sunday school, to state its purpose and to relate to the St Agnes area. Nicola Williams won the prize for her design which included a view of St Agnes Beacon. The job of making it passed to Miss Hopkins and Miss Lack who undertook it free of charge.

The Classes of the 1980s and 1990s

In 1980 a Shell Club was formed, a youth club for children aged seven to ten. The hope was that it would help to strengthen the junior department of the Sunday school. Ian Jones and Miss Alison Oates were joint leaders and Alan Gray was Secretary.

In 1982 Mrs Betty Heyworth resigned her position as Treasurer having been in the role since 1954 – that's a lot of adding up. The following year there was another retirement when Miss Elsie Vanstone stood down. She was the Sunday school's longest serving teacher and in appreciation of her tremendous contribution she was presented with an album of photographs.

In 1983 Glynis Teagle (née Olds) took on the post of Superintendent. She had regularly attended Sunday school since the age of three and had become a teacher in 1964, having started as an assistant to the long-serving Elsie Vanstone. In 1971 Glynis became the leader of the Primary Department.

During the 1980s the membership increased; junior and senior youth clubs were opened and flourished. For the first time in many years the senior department of the Sunday school included a large number of teenagers. More space was needed – a problem but a pleasant one. The Worship Centre designed in the 1964 re-construction had, for various reasons, never been fully used and had become a storeroom. Plans were drawn up to bring it into use. The new-look room was opened in 1986 providing a comfortable area for worship by the junior and senior departments of the Sunday school; it was also used as a smaller, informal area for evening services.

In 1984 it was the 175th anniversary and to celebrate the milestone an eight-day "week" of events was planned: Clive Benney presented a display of village postcards, Bill and Esther Cheshire organised a walking treasure hunt/barbecue and, of course, there was the inevitable traditional tea treat. The services on the first and last Sunday sandwiched the events which were supported by ex-ministers the Revds Joe Ridholls, Raymond Foster and Philip Williams. There were also some presentations: as a mark of their considerable achievement Mrs Phyllis Pharoah (1935 to 1976), Miss Elsie Vanstone (1951 to 1983) and Mrs June Lovering (1953 to date) were presented with Long Service Certificates.

In 1985 Sunday school Superintendent Glynis Teagle led the large team of 15 teachers and helpers who presided over a Sunday school which, by now, comprised 94 regular members – 38 primary and beginners, 35 juniors and 21 young people.

In 1986, Chapel Treasurer David Teagle pleaded for extra funds to cover the cost of a new heating system. The young members were keen to give their support and responded by holding a car wash (described as a lively if rather wet morning) and a coffee morning. There was also a 24-hour sponsored disco in aid of the MacMillan Relief Fund, referred to as, "a seemingly endless, noisy experience." But no doubt it was worthwhile.

In 1987 there was a healthy Sunday school and an active Junior and Senior Youth Club, but the arrival of a new minister from America brought further energy and excitement. Although the Revd Steven Emery was able to connect with all ages, he had a love and real passion for youth work. His enthusiasm, sense of fun and powerful preaching had a great effect on the teaching staff, the children, the teenagers and their families.

The youth programme was wide and varied. Large numbers attended on Sunday mornings and the teenagers also met on Wednesday and Friday nights. The juniors continued to enjoy a wide range of activities at their youth club on Friday nights. Two Youth Fellowship Groups were formed and met on Sunday nights: one at the home of Glynis and David Teagle led by Christine Roberts and Glynis, and the other at the Chapel, led by Steven Emery-Wright. These were very strong groups and in 1989/1990 resulted in 18 young people being accepted into full membership of the Methodist Church.

By 1989 there were over 50 young people in the seniors alone and 90 attending the youth clubs and so it was decided to bring the whole youth programme under one umbrella. The Sunday school took the form of a Junior Sunday Group under its leader, Mrs Elaine Randall, and a Senior Sunday Morning Youth Department under Mrs Christine Roberts.

By now, Glynis Teagle had moved from the position of Sunday school Superintendent to the newly formed post of Youth Co-ordinator. In this role she presided over a Youth Council made up of leaders of the various departments. The youth clubs were thriving under the leadership of Glynis, Christine Roberts, Pam Williams, David Teagle, Mary Laity, Janet Rafferty, Joyce Hocking, Helen Gay and Youth Choir musicians David Barker and Terri White. There were 54 seniors and 36 juniors, a total membership of 90.

In 1990 Steven Emery-Wright was due to leave, to return to America, and the members of the Youth Section wanted to show their appreciation of his enthusiastic support. They organised a 4th of July American style Barn Dance at Porthtowan and David Teagle somehow managed to keep the secret from him as he drove him there.

The October 1990 newsletter reflected that Mrs Daphne Matthews, Mrs June Lovering and Bill Cheshire had jointly given 100 years of service to the Sunday school. After their long periods of loyal work they were stepping down.

In 1994 an after-school club for children aged five to seven was formed. 'Bounce' was held on Friday afternoons and large numbers came bounding through the doors during the first few weeks. Marilyn Shears and Glynis Teagle ran this happy little club of 45 members.

All of the groups within St Agnes Methodist Church Youth Department were represented at the Annual General Meeting on the 16th June 1997 when the agenda included a challenging item, that the Church in America and Britain had almost lost the opportunity and ability to speak and communicate the Gospel message to the young people of today. It concluded that various new ways and technology needed to be promoted for outreach in a modern society.

During the Chapel alterations in 1998 the classes were held in the Women's Institute and in the same year Janet Rafferty (née Olds) celebrated 30 years as a Sunday school teacher. She would continue for a further five years and finish in 2003: during the latter stages she took over the reins as leader – effectively the Sunday school Superintendent.

The District and Beyond

In August 1988 many members joined other Cornish children in a summer camp at the Royal Cornwall Showground. They made quite an impression as they made their entrance in yellow sweatshirts.

In the same year Glynis Teagle was appointed Cornwall Methodist District Youth and Children's Secretary and the members of the Sunday school and youth clubs began to attend more District events including camps, activity days, rallies and the very popular national event – the MAYC (Methodist Association of Youth Clubs) London Weekend. Glynis said, "For several years the teenagers travelled to London for this event. In May of each year, thousands of Methodist youngsters from all over the country merged on London to have fun, 'sleep' on church floors, share a time of fellowship, take part in a walk of witness and attend a service in the Royal Albert Hall. I have many wonderful memories of these weekends, two in particular. Sarah White, one of the teenagers booked to attend the event, broke her leg a few weeks before the weekend. She was so upset at the thought of not going that the group pledged to look after her for the weekend, not really thinking about how she was going to get around London – after all, she had her crutches and a wheelchair. As a result, one of the leaders, David Teagle, had the task of carrying her up and down the numerous escalators and steps of the many underground stations en route to our destinations. Taking 33 teenagers from Cornwall to London is no mean feat, particularly when it comes to guiding them around the city. Everything has to be done with military precision. So on a Saturday afternoon, in a busy Oxford Street, I bundled them onto a bus just in time for it to move off – quite an achievement. But then I looked out of the back window and saw a frantic and panic-struck Christine Roberts, my fellow leader, waving like mad. We had left her behind on the pavement. At the next stop we all had to clamber off the bus and go back to meet her."

Teams performed well in the various District quizzes and St Agnes hosted several Circuit and District youth events; on one occasion the then MAYC Connexional Secretary, the Revd Dave Martin, was the leader.

During the eighties and early nineties the young people enjoyed several group holidays and for many years they travelled with Christine and Brian Roberts to Diss in Norfolk. The young people slept on the floor of Diss Methodist Church, enjoyed a week of sight-seeing and assisted Christine in the worship on the Sunday morning. Glynis and David Teagle also organised holidays to the Lake District, the Peak District and to Brixham. These were slightly more adventurous with abseiling, rock climbing and canoeing in the week's programme. The evenings were spent having fun in group activities, lively discussion and a short act of worship. Both groups were well supported by strong teams of adult volunteers who helped with driving the mini buses, cooking and cleaning up.

The New Millennium

At the 2002 AGM Janet Rafferty reported that the number attending Sunday school had decreased slightly, it varied between eight to sixteen children. The minutes record that there had been no Youth Club during the year and it was agreed to place its funds in a deposit account.

At the meeting the following year the Revd Beverley Hollings stated that some of the existing teachers were stepping down; she thanked them for their long and loyal service. There were 20 young people attending Sunday school and she considered that it was time to look at new or alternative methods of running the Youth Department. There was also a reminder of the need to ensure that all persons working with children and young people need to comply with child protection regulations.

The Revd Joan and Tony Watson began "The Gap" in January 2007, helped by parents and church members. It was an after-school club for secondary school children offering a range of activities but it closed in March 2008 owing to lack of support.

Since 2003 Diane Read and Pat Carr have run the Sunday Club with help from Dinah Teagle, Linda Harding, Doreen Meloy, Doreen Ritchie, June Lovering, Joyce Trevethan, Jenny Osborne and Marilyn Shears. Diane takes care of about a dozen toddlers and juniors and at the age of eleven they move to the senior group under Pat Carr. Pat's group currently consists of eight youngsters, all boys, who meet in the morning and enjoy a breakfast before involving themselves in a variety of activities.

The Skateboard club, "Variel," now meets after school on the 2nd and 4th Friday of the month. Claire Newby and Tim Hibbins, Youth Leaders from Perranporth, started it in 2008 and Pat Carr, Ron and Doreen Meloy, William Trevethan, Tim Hibbins and the Revd Joan Watson now lead it. The activity takes place in the Chapel grounds, near the coffee lounge. It is directed at secondary school children and during the winter months there are alternative indoor activities including Wii, PS3 games, bar football and table tennis.

Claire Newby, Perranporth and St Agnes Youth Worker, runs "Youth Cell." This meets on the 2nd, 4th and 5th Monday of each month and is an opportunity for young people of secondary school age to share a meal and explore the Bible.

The Revd Joan Watson is generous in her praise of those working with the young people. She said, "The leaders have my admiration. In 2006, young people attending Sunday Club were at an all time low, down to single figures, but under the leadership of Pat Carr, Diane Read and their team of willing helpers, the number began to rise and now, in 2009, we have 25 young people on the books with about 18 attending regularly. That includes several teenage boys. In a time when the majority of churches have no children at all we are doing very well, especially where the teenage lads are concerned."

It was back in 1809 that the Sunday school first started, 200 years ago. In 2009 it celebrated its bi-centenary and to commemorate the occasion Glynis Teagle presented a superb display of its history. The photographs and records brought back memories for many people and the event was so well received that it was repeated during St Agnes Carnival Week.

The Youth Department today is perhaps a far cry from the days when the membership could be counted in hundreds but the commitment to involve the young people in the Methodist Church and to teach them Christian values is as strong as ever. This chapter is a tribute to the many people, past and present, who have given their time and talents to provide thousands of St Agnes children with a solid foundation for their future life. It may well be that many of the youngsters no longer take an active part in church life here but most will undoubtedly have retained the values and ideals that they first learned at St Agnes Methodist Sunday school.

Past, Present and Future

By Betty Tredinnick

As might be expected, the proliferation of different branches, or strands, of Methodism in the 19th century led in some places to a certain divisiveness and sometimes antagonism even within Methodism itself, so it is perhaps not surprising that relations between church and chapel were generally cool and sometimes acrimonious – as when a St Agnes vicar in the early 20th century told a prominent chapel member that he would never set foot in "that place" – meaning the chapel! In an age when most people attended a place of worship, the population tended to be quite rigidly divided, with only occasional transferences of allegiance if a family became dissatisfied with their previous religious home. However, during the century attitudes gradually changed and no longer was the "other place" unfavourably commented on, and of course, there were always some families and more broadminded folk who bridged the gap with their personal friendships.

Perhaps one can say that the ministry of the Vicar, the Revd Michael Williamson (1973-1986), marked the beginning of closer ties and a changing attitude as he encouraged an ecumenical discussion group which met at the home of John and Glanville Briney. During his ministry the first ecumenical tea treat was held in 1978, as mentioned earlier. He also broke new ground by inviting a woman local Preacher to preach at the Parish Church on Palm Sunday 1986, commenting wryly afterwards, "Well Miss Tredinnick, the roof has not fallen in!" He became a great personal friend of the then Methodist minister, the Revd Graham Caink – a friendship which has lasted until the present day, despite the removal of both of them far from St Agnes.

In 1987 when the Revd Steven Emery had just arrived from America, he was invited to attend the Institution of Revd Michael Adams as the new Vicar and to welcome him on behalf of the Methodists. This he did with great aplomb and in a highly exaggerated Cornish accent, much to the amusement of the Bishop. That service marked another stage in the closer co-operation between the clergy which was further enhanced when the Revd Gerry Wallis was Methodist minister. During his three-month sabbatical and occasionally when he was ill, Fr Michael took the Wednesday morning Communion service at the chapel, and he also invited the Methodists to hold this Service in the parish church during the alterations of 1998.

A new impetus was given to ecumenical relations with the Institution of the Revd Alan Bashforth in April 2001: under his leadership an Ecumenical Discussion Group was started – a monthly gathering of 20-30 folk from all the three churches in the village to hear and discuss with speakers of some distinction in various fields of study.

From at least 1992 onwards there have been regular meetings of clergy and lay representatives of all the churches in St Agnes – Anglican, Methodists and Roman Catholic. These have arranged all the united and special Services throughout the year: Remembrance Sunday when the Service alternates between the Parish Church and the Methodist, the Good Friday Walk of Witness beginning at the Chapel and ending with a short Service in the Square, sometimes a united Service on Easter Day, a united Service during Carnival Week either on the beach or in the grounds of the Chapel, Harvest Festivals at both the Anglican and Methodist churches, a united Christingle on Christmas Eve, again alternating between the Anglican and Methodist churches as the Roman Catholic church is too small to accommodate such Services. During the last decade there has also been an annual Ecumenical Supper when members of all three churches come together during the Week of Prayer for Christian Unity for food, fun and fellowship.

From at least 1992 until 2008 there were also united evening services once a month at each of the three churches in turn but, as these were not particularly well attended of late, it was felt that united morning services would be more meaningful as most people attended those. So, beginning in January 2009, there was a united Covenant Service at the Methodist church followed a few weeks later by a united Service for Feast Sunday at the Parish church. As both of these are eucharistic services, this change signalled a further stage on the road to closer collaboration – a road which saw a more marked and important milestone on Feast Sunday 2010 when in the presence of the Bishop of Truro, the Rt Revd Tim Thornton, and the Chair of the Methodist District, the Revd Steve Wild, a Declaration of Intent to work even more closely together was signed by the clergy and lay representatives of both churches.

Visually, the greatest change to the interior of the chapel came in the 1964 alterations with the removal of the vast and ornate rostrum and its replacement by a side pulpit (and later lectern as well) and a central Communion Table. As "structures speak messages," this change has certainly signified a greater emphasis on Communion Services over the past 45 years, while the Cross on the Table would certainly have been viewed by some folk during the 1920s and 1930s as a sign almost of idolatry! From being an optional extra Service in the earlier days of the 20th century, following the main preaching service, the Communion Service when held is now an integral part of the main one. And from being a Lenten Service introduced by the Revd Steven Emery in 1988, the Wednesday morning Communion Service has become regular and much appreciated ever since. This greater emphasis on sacramental worship would, one feels, please our father in God, John Wesley, who bade his early followers continue attendance at their parish church for Holy Communion as well as going to their local meeting house or chapel for

Methodist worship and preaching. I feel sure too, that as one who said he would live and die an Anglican he would rejoice at the greater understanding, friendship and co-operation with Anglicans signalled by the recent signing of the Declaration of Intent.

l-r; Diane Willoughby, Ordinand, the Chair of the Cornwall District, the Revd Steve Wild, Revd Joan Watson, the Bishop of Truro, the Rt Revd Tim Thornton and Revd Alan Bashforth in January 2010.

From at least the latter part of the 19th century it seems that the new chapel dominated the lives of most of its members, for it was their social centre as well as their spiritual home. Young and old spent many hours there, attending weeknight meetings as well as Sunday Services, practising for concerts and plays or providing the teas or suppers which inevitably followed all entertainment and major events – the Boxing Day concert, the concert on Feast Monday after the afternoon Service in the chapel, the choir giving one of the shorter oratorios on Good Friday. The word "outreach" was unknown then, but there was little need of it when most people in the village were involved in the activities of church or chapel. However, as the 20th century wore on and the two World Wars brought greater mobility, enforced or chosen, into the lives of more people, church-going declined and with it the dominance of church or chapel activities over the whole of life. So how in the early 21st century are Methodists to obey John Wesley's command to "go not to those who need you but to those who need you most"? It is, of course, a most demanding behest which few of us would say we have fully obeyed. However, all the various activities and groups now using chapel premises or sponsored by the chapel – and the great expenditure to provide its facilities – are, we hope, signs of our attempts to provide some of that outreach. As one who provided education, medicine and many other practical forms of help for the poor and needy in his own day, as well as visiting the sick and prisoners, John Wesley would, we hope, approve of our modern interpretation of mission, and of the many enterprises his followers here have undertaken over the past centuries to help provide companionship and food – both physical and spiritual – not only for members but for the community at large.

This book has attempted to trace the history of Methodism over the past 250 years in this very small part of John Wesley's "world parish," and particularly as shown in the 150 years of the present chapel's existence. Since their peak in late 19th century and early 20th century, congregations have declined here, as elsewhere in this country, and some gloomy forecasts have predicted that in another 20 years Methodism will cease to exist. Be that as it may, despite fewer members and adherents, we hope that regardless of denominational labels, Mr Wesley's "parishioners" will possess what he called "the catholic spirit which embraces with a strong and cordial affection neighbours and strangers, friends and enemies, and give their hand to all whose hearts are right with their heart," in the service of our Lord.

Appendix

Wesleyan Methodist Ministers of St Agnes Circuit
compiled by Bill Morrison from Baptismal Registers

1837	Thomas Jewell		1874	Robert Burdon
1837	Peter Parsons		1874	Ebenezer Moulton
1839	John Dawson		1876	Joseph Robert Warburton
1839	Elias Thomas		1877	Philip Callier
1841	Joseph Fletcher		1877	Joseph Nield
1841	John Hanson		1877	David Eyne or Eyre
1842	John Cullen		1878	Jabez Overton
1842	John Shaw		1878	William H Weatherill
1844	John Bissell		1880	Stephen James Little
1846	Elijah Toyne		1880	Robert Daw
1848	James Pilley		1882	John S Vickers
1850	Henry Young		1883	John T Bennett
1851	William D Tyack		1884	Richard Webb
1853	Joseph Whitehead		1886	William Heddon Major
1854	John Jeffreys		1888	W Rhode Davies
1854	Frederick C Haine or Haime		1889	Charles Roberts
1855	H B Trethewey		1890	John Lamplough
1856	Robert Mainwaring		1891	John Preston
1857	Peter Parsons		1894	Edward Harris
1858	William H W Evans		1895	Joseph Milligan
1860	Henry Daniels		1898	George Reid
1860	Robert C Barratt		1899	Richard Hill
1862	Robert George Badcock		1902	R Corlette Cowell **
1863	Christopher Ridler		1902	??? Ackroyd **
1864	Alfred Barber		1903	G W Thompson
1864	William Hopkins		1906	William G Corke
1865	Jabez Overton		1909	William Rider
1867	Aaron Edman		1912	Sylvester Lee
1868	Frederick Hunter		1915	Thomas Hosking and John J Barton
1870	Joseph Henry Skewes		1919	C W Hickson
1870	Peter Prescott		1920	Frank E Poad
1873	Charles Symes		1923	H Taylor

1926	J E Knox	1962	Raymond J Foster
1929	R W Taylor	1969	Philip D Williams
1930	William Ball	1974	Kenneth R Sadler
1932	Francis G Gray	1979	Graham Caink
1934	A Trevellick Cape	1986	Stephen Normanton
1937	A G Payne	1987	Steven Emery-Wright
1939	H T Dixon	1990	John Haley
1943	William Norman Warren	1994	Gerald Wallis
1946	F J Le Poidevin	1999	Beverly Hollings
1949	Frank A White	2005	Martha Caputo
1953	Ambrose W J Payne	2006	Joan Watson
1957	Joseph A D Ridholls		

** Referred to only by "The Cornish Post and Mining News"

Sunday school Superintendents from 1934 to 1990

1934	Mr Maddison
1935 - 1937	Reg Roberts and E M Uglow
1938 - 1939	E M Uglow
1940 - 1945	Reg Roberts
1946 - 1950	Noel Hoskins
1951 - 1956	Bill Morrison
1957	vacant at AGM
1958 - 1964	Bill Morrison
1965	Mrs Margaret Hoskins
1966	Roger James
1967	Mrs Christine Morrison
1968	Mrs June Lovering
1969	Mrs Margaret Hoskins and Mrs Christine Morrison
1970	Mrs Daphne Matthews
1971	Mrs June Lovering
1972 - 1974	Mrs Christine Morrison
1975 - 1981	David Rees
1981 - 1983	Mrs Denise Rogers
1984 - 1988	Mrs Glynis Teagle
1989 - 1990	Mrs Elaine Randall
Role discontinued	

Sunday school Secretaries from 1934 to 1992

1934 - 1935	W A Butson
1936 - 1937	W A Butson and L Stephens
1938 - 1940	W A Butson
1941 - 1942	W A Butson and J Solomon
1943 - 1944	H Butcher and D Roberts
1945 - 1946	Margaret Davey
1947	Mrs Thelma Bunt
1948 - 1952	Miss Betty Hocking
1953 - 1954	Mrs B Blewett (née Hocking)
1955 - 1957	Miss Marlene Skewes
1958 - 1961	Mrs Butcher
1962 - 1965	Mrs Davey
1966 - 1967	Miss Janet Hoskins
1968 - 1971	Miss Glynis Olds
1972 - 1973	Miss Mary Morrison
1974 - 1983	Mrs Dinah Teagle
1984 - 1988	Mrs Janet Rafferty
1989	Vacant at AGM
1990 - 1992	Mrs Rosemary James

Sunday school Treasurers from 1934 to 2003

1934 - 1942	C Pope
1943	F E Dunstan
1944 - 1945	C Pope
1946	Miss Mabel Trezise
1947	Miss Betty Hocking
1948 - 1949	Percy James
1950	Paul James
1951 - 1953	Mrs Thelma Bunt
1954 - 1981	Miss Betty Hellyar / Mrs Betty Heyworth
1982 - 1984	Mrs Kathleen Woolcock (née Morrison)
1985 - 1986	Miss Bridget Nankivell
1987 - 1988	Miss L Springall
1989 - 2003	Mrs Alison Jones (née Williams)

Acknowledgements

We are pleased to acknowledge the help we have received with our research, particularly from the following people:

Mike Ashmore
John Bathe
Donald Blight
Margaret Bonner
Colin Butson
Pat Carr
Margaret Davey
Revd David Easton
Ralph Fowler
Ron and Pam George
Margaret Hoskins
John Jotcham
Anne Knight
Claire Murton of The St Agnes Museum Trust
Hilary Nankivell

Jenny Osborne
David Rees
Revd Joe Ridholls
Frank and Pam Roberts
Malcolm Rogers
Richard Sandercock
Joan Shaw
Peter Simmons
Dinah Teagle
Glynis Teagle
Tom Thompson
Betty Tredinnick
Elizabeth Thorley
Revd Joan Watson
Revd Philip Williams

Our special thanks go to those people who have been so generous in giving their time to make this book possible: to the Revd Joe Ridholls for his guiding hand, the Church Steering Committee of Derek Skinner, Brian Roberts, Glynis Teagle, Betty Tredinnick and the Revd Joan Watson with particular mention of Betty who led the group, contributed to the written work and undertook the proof reading.

A noted local Methodist, the Revd Thomas Shaw died in May 2001. The Methodist Church lost a gifted minister and a dedicated Methodist historian. His work has been quoted in many religious and non-religious books and we are pleased to have been able to "borrow" from it for this and in a number of our other publications.

The archive photographs appearing in this book are from many sources including the late Bill Morrison and the Clive Benney Collection.

Our research has been greatly helped by the excellent staff of the Cornish Studies Library, the Courtney Library, the Cornwall County Records Office and the St Agnes Museum Trust; these are invaluable sources of information for local historians.

References

Brief History of Methodism in Cornwall by
The Revd David Easton

Friendly Retreat by Maurice Bizley

How to get methodical with your Cornish Methodists by the
Revd Colin C Short

Jack of all Trades by W (Bill) H Morrison

Journals of the St Agnes Museum Trust **

Methodist Chapels in the Parish of St Agnes compiled by
Frank Carpenter **

Methodist Clergy in St Agnes by W (Bill) H Morrison **

Methodism in St Agnes (paper) by W (Bill) H Morrison

Parish Chapels (paper) by the Revd David Easton

St Agnes Wesleyan Chapel leaders minute book
1883 to 1944

The St Agnes Wesleyan Chapel Treasurer's account book

Souvenir programme of 1964 by the Revd Raymond Foster

The Next Chapter Cornish Methodism 1965 – 2005 by the
Revd Ian Haile

St Agnes Methodist Church Newsletters

** by kind permission of St Agnes Museum Trust

Newspapers

The Cornish Post and Mining News
The Royal Cornwall Gazette
The Sherborne Mercury
The West Briton

Books written by the same authors

Clive Benney

St Agnes Parish 1850 to 1920 A photographic record
St Agnes Parish 1920 to 1950 A photographic record
Around St Agnes…The Archive Photographic Series
St Agnes…A Photographic History Volume 1 Down Quay
St Agnes…A Photographic History Volume 2 Village and Shops
St Agnes…A Photographic History Volume 3 Down to Dirty Pool

Tony Mansell

Mithian in the Parishes of St Agnes and Perranzabuloe
St Agnes and its Band
Camborne Town Band
St Agnes Golf Society

Clive Benney and Tony Mansell

A History of Blackwater and its Neighbours
Jericho to Cligga
Our Village Church
Memories of Mount Hawke